Contents

PUMPKIN BREAD..
CHRISTMAS BREAKFAST SAUSAGE CASSEROLE...
FRENCH TOAST ....
PUMPKIN BREAD.. 8
BAKED FRENCH TOAST... 9
BANANA BREAD 10
FRENCH TOAST CASSEROLE 10
EASY PANCAKES... 11
QUICK QUICHE 11
EASY BROCCOLI QUICHE 12
IRRESISTIBLE IRISH SODA BREAD 13
TODD'S FAMOUS BLUEBERRY PANCAKES 13
MEGAN'S GRANOLA 14
CATHY'S BANANA BREAD 15
PANCAKESS.. 16
SAUSAGE CASSEROLE 16
SAUSAGE BALLS 17
CINNAMON BREAD.. 17
ZUCCHINI BREAD 18
CREPES 19
DESSERT CREPES 19
MOM'S BUTTERMILK PANCAKES 20
TRUCK-STOP BUTTERMILK PANCAKES... 20
CREME BRULEE FRENCH TOAST 21
OLD CHARLESTON STYLE SHRIMP AND GRITS 22
OLD-FASHIONED PANCAKES 23
OATMEAL PANCAKES 24
EASY QUICHE 24
EGG AND SAUSAGE CASSEROLE 25
PANCAKES 25
BAKED OATMEAL 26
EASY SAUSAGE GRAVY AND BISCUITS 27

1

WHOLE GRAIN WAFFLES	27
VANILLA CREPES	28
GERMAN POTATO PANCAKES	29
VEGAN PANCAKES	29
BACON FOR THE FAMILY OR A CROWD	30
BAKED HAM AND CHEESE PARTY SANDWICHES	30
UGLIES	31
LIGHT AND FLUFFY SPINACH QUICHE	31
WHOLE WHEAT BLUEBERRY PANCAKES	32
BREAKFAST PIES	33
EASY BANANA BREAD	33
FRENCH CREPES	34
DUTCH BABIES	34
OVEN SCRAMBLED EGGS	35
CHARLESTON BREAKFAST CASSEROLE	36
EASY BACON AND CHEESE QUICHE	36
DELICIOUS PUMPKIN BREAD	37
SCRAMBLED EGGS DONE RIGHT	38
SPINACH AND POTATO FRITTATA	38
BUTTERMILK PANCAKES	39
BUTTERSCOTCH OATMEAL	39
BAKED DENVER OMELET	40
EASTER BREAKFAST CASSEROLE	40
PUMPKIN PIE BREAD	41
CRAB QUICHE	42
SPINACH QUICHE WITH COTTAGE CHEESE	42
FRENCH TOAST	43
EGGS BENEDICT	43
LOLA'S HORCHATA	44
QUICK AND EASY HOME FRIES	45
BREAKFAST CASSEROLE	45
WHEAT GERM WHOLE-WHEAT BUTTERMILK PANCAKES	46
APPLE BREAKFAST BREAD	47
MAKE AHEAD FRENCH TOAST	47

ASPARAGUS QUICHE	48
OATMEAL AND WHEAT FLOUR BLUEBERRY PANCAKES	49
QUICHE	49
WAFFLES	50
MOM'S BEST WAFFLES	51
CHRISTMAS BRUNCH CASSEROLE	51
CHUNKY MONKEY PANCAKES	52
GERMAN PANCAKES	53
BROWN SUGAR BANANA NUT BREAD	53
LOWER FAT BANANA BREAD	54
BAKED OMELET	55
EASY SPICY ROASTED POTATOES	55
APPLE RAISIN FRENCH TOAST STRATA	56
EGG IN A HOLE	57
WHOLE WHEAT, OATMEAL, AND BANANA PANCAKES	57
MOM'S APPLESAUCE PANCAKES	58
BAKED OATMEAL	58
BANANA NUT BREAD	59
APPLE-RAISIN FRENCH TOAST CASSEROLE	60
ORANGE PECAN FRENCH TOAST	60
VERONICA'S APPLE PANCAKES	61
QUICHE LORRAINE	62
BACON QUICHE TARTS	63
OMELET IN A BAG	63
GRAIN AND NUT WHOLE WHEAT PANCAKES	64
BANANA PEANUT BUTTER BREAD	65
FLUFFY AND DELICIOUS PANCAKES	65
TENDER AND EASY BUTTERMILK WAFFLES	66
SUNSHINE TOAST	67
LOUISIANA SWEET POTATO PANCAKES	67
MAKE AHEAD BREAKFAST CASSEROLE	68
AMAZING MUFFIN CUPS	69
EASY QUICHE LORRAINE	69
INDIVIDUAL BAKED EGGS	70

BAKED OMELET ROLL	71
JOSEPH'S BEST EASY BACON RECIPE	71
TATER TOT CASSEROLE	72
POTATO SKILLET	72
COUNTRY QUICHE	73
PEANUT BUTTER AND BANANA FRENCH TOAST	74
SCRAMBLED EGG MUFFINS	74
MONKEY BREAD	75
HASH BROWN QUICHE	75
RICH AND DELICIOUS BANANA BREAD	76
FRENCH TOAST SOUFFLE	77
LOWER FAT BANANA BREAD	77
OVERNIGHT APPLE CINNAMON FRENCH TOAST	78
FLUFFY CANADIAN PANCAKES	79
PUMPKIN WAFFLES WITH APPLE CIDER SYRUP	79
CREAMY STRAWBERRY CREPES	80
CINNAMON GRIDDLE CAKES	81
IRISH SODA BREAD	82
PEACH FRENCH TOAST	82
BREAKFAST CASSEROLE	83
BABY SPINACH OMELET	84
HONEY NUT GRANOLA	84
HAM AND CHEESE QUICHE	85
STOVETOP GRANOLA	86
STRAWBERRY VANILLA PANCAKES	86
ZUCCHINI BREAD	87
FAST AND EASY PANCAKES	88
BANANA CREPES	88
CRAB QUICHE	89
MY-HOP PANCAKES	90
PUMPKIN PANCAKES	90
WHOLE WHEAT PANCAKES	91
OATMEAL BANANA NUT BREAD	92
SAUSAGE BRUNCH CASSEROLE	93

BAKED OMELET SQUARES	93
FARMER'S CASSEROLE	94
SUNDAY MORNING LEMON POPPY SEED PANCAKES	95
MONTE CRISTO SANDWICH - THE REAL ONE	96
BRUNCH ENCHILADAS	96
HOME-FRIED POTATOES	97
BLUEBERRY FRENCH TOAST	98
CLASSIC HASH BROWNS	99
BAKED PUMPKIN BREAD	99
EMMA'S BELGIAN WAFFLES	100
BANANA BREAD	100
CHAKCHOUKA (SHAKSHOUKA)	101
BAKED EGGS	102
QUICK ALMOND FLOUR PANCAKES	102
COUNTRY STYLE FRIED POTATOES	103
KIELBASA AND POTATO BAKE	103
DOMINICAN STYLE OATMEAL	104
SHRIMP AND GRITS	105
BREAKFAST PIZZA	106
HAM AND CHEESE BREAKFAST QUICHE	106
PUMPKIN SPICED LATTE	107
CREAMED EGGS ON TOAST	107
CRAB AND SWISS QUICHE	108
EGG AND HASH BROWN PIE	109
AUTHENTIC MEXICAN BREAKFAST TACOS	109
PEAR BREAD	110
QUICK AND EASY MONKEY BREAD	111
OVERNIGHT FRENCH TOAST	111
SAUSAGE CRESCENT ROLLS	112
EASY SWEDISH PANCAKES	113
EXTRA-YUMMY FLUFFY PANCAKES	113
DELICIOUS GLUTEN-FREE PANCAKES	114
ULTIMATE BREAKFAST CASSEROLE	115
BROCCOLI QUICHE WITH MASHED POTATO CRUST	115

PALEO OMELET MUFFINS 116
GREAT EASY WAFFLES 117
SUPER EASY EGG CASSEROLE 117

PUMPKIN BREAD

Servings: 36 | Prep: 15m | Cooks: 1h | Total: 1h15m

NUTRITION FACTS

Calories: 247 | Carbohydrates: 36.8g | Fat: 10.3g | Protein: 3g | Cholesterol: 31mg

INGREDIENTS

- 3 cups canned pumpkin puree
- 1 1/2 teaspoons baking soda
- 1 1/2 cups vegetable oil
- 1 1/2 teaspoons salt
- 4 cups white sugar
- 1 1/2 teaspoons ground cinnamon
- 6 eggs
- 1 1/2 teaspoons ground nutmeg
- 4 3/4 cups all-purpose flour
- 1 1/2 teaspoons ground cloves
- 1 1/2 teaspoons baking powder

DIRECTIONS

1. Preheat the oven to 350 degrees F (175 degrees C). Grease and flour three 9x5 inch loaf pans
2. In a large bowl, mix together the pumpkin, oil, sugar, and eggs. Combine the flour, baking powder, baking soda, salt, cinnamon, nutmeg, and cloves; stir into the pumpkin mixture until well blended. Divide the batter evenly between the prepared pans.
3. Bake in preheated oven for 45 minutes to 1 hour. The top of the loaf should spring back when lightly pressed.

CHRISTMAS BREAKFAST SAUSAGE CASSEROLE

Servings: 8 | Prep: 20m | Cooks: 1h30m | Total: 9h50m | Additional: 8h

NUTRITION FACTS

Calories: 377 | Carbohydrates: 13.4g | Fat: 26g | Protein: 21.5g | Cholesterol: 160mg

INGREDIENTS

- 1 pound ground pork sausage
- 2 cups milk
- 1 teaspoon mustard powder
- 6 slices white bread, toasted and cut into cubes

- 1/2 teaspoon salt
- 8 ounces mild Cheddar cheese, shredded
- 4 eggs, beaten

DIRECTIONS

1. Crumble sausage into a medium skillet. Cook over medium heat until evenly brown; drain.
2. In a medium bowl, mix together mustard powder, salt, eggs and milk. Add the sausage, bread cubes, and cheese, and stir to coat evenly. Pour into a greased 9x13 inch baking dish. Cover, and chill in the refrigerator for 8 hours, or overnight.
3. Preheat oven to 350 degrees F (175 degrees C).
4. Cover, and bake 45 to 60 minutes. Uncover, and reduce temperature to 325 degrees F (165 degrees C). Bake for an additional 30 minutes, or until set.

FRENCH TOAST

Servings: 3 | Prep: 5m | Cooks: 15m | Total: 20m

NUTRITION FACTS

Calories: 240 | Carbohydrates: 33.6g | Fat: 6.4g | Protein: 10.6g | Cholesterol: 128mg

INGREDIENTS

- 6 thick slices bread
- 1/4 teaspoon ground nutmeg (optional)
- 2 eggs
- 1 teaspoon vanilla extract (optional)
- 2/3 cup milk
- salt to taste
- 1/4 teaspoon ground cinnamon (optional)

DIRECTIONS

1. Beat together egg, milk, salt, desired spices and vanilla.
2. Heat a lightly oiled griddle or skillet over medium-high heat.
3. Dunk each slice of bread in egg mixture, soaking both sides. Place in pan, and cook on both sides until golden. Serve hot.

PUMPKIN BREAD

Servings: 36 | Prep: 15m | Cooks: 1h | Total: 1h15m

NUTRITION FACTS

Calories: 247 | Carbohydrates: 36.8g | Fat: 10.3g | Protein: 3g | Cholesterol: 31mg

INGREDIENTS

- 3 cups canned pumpkin puree
- 1 1/2 teaspoons baking soda
- 1 1/2 cups vegetable oil
- 1 1/2 teaspoons salt
- 4 cups white sugar
- 1 1/2 teaspoons ground cinnamon
- 6 eggs
- 1 1/2 teaspoons ground nutmeg
- 4 3/4 cups all-purpose flour
- 1 1/2 teaspoons ground cloves
- 1 1/2 teaspoons baking powder

DIRECTIONS

1. Preheat the oven to 350 degrees F (175 degrees C). Grease and flour three 9x5 inch loaf pans.
2. In a large bowl, mix together the pumpkin, oil, sugar, and eggs. Combine the flour, baking powder, baking soda, salt, cinnamon, nutmeg, and cloves; stir into the pumpkin mixture until well blended. Divide the batter evenly between the prepared pans.
3. Bake in preheated oven for 45 minutes to 1 hour. The top of the loaf should spring back when lightly pressed.

BAKED FRENCH TOAST

Servings: 12 | Prep: 15m | Cooks: 40m | Total: 15h

NUTRITION FACTS

Calories: 395 | Carbohydrates: 44.4g | Fat: 19.8g | Protein: 11g | Cholesterol: 169mg

INGREDIENTS

- 1 (1 pound) loaf French bread, cut diagonally in 1 inch slices
- 1/4 teaspoon ground cinnamon
- 8 eggs
- 3/4 cup butter
- 2 cups milk
- 1 1/3 cups brown sugar
- 1 1/2 cups half-and-half cream
- 3 tablespoons light corn syrup

- 2 teaspoons vanilla extract

DIRECTIONS

1. Butter a 9x13 inch baking dish. Arrange the slices of bread in the bottom. In a large bowl, beat together eggs, milk, cream, vanilla and cinnamon. Pour over bread slices, cover, and refrigerate overnight.
2. The next morning, preheat oven to 350 degrees F (175 degrees C). In a small saucepan, combine butter, brown sugar and corn syrup; heat until bubbling. Pour over bread and egg mixture.
3. Bake in preheated oven, uncovered, for 40 minutes.

BANANA BREAD

Servings: 16 | Prep: 15m | Cooks: 1h | Total: 1h15m

NUTRITION FACTS

Calories: 145 | Carbohydrates: 26.5g | Fat: 3.7g | Protein: 2.3g | Cholesterol: 31mg

INGREDIENTS

- 1 1/2 cups all-purpose flour
- 2 eggs, beaten
- 1 teaspoon baking soda
- 1/4 cup butter, melted
- 1/2 teaspoon salt
- 3 bananas, mashed
- 1 cup white sugar

DIRECTIONS

1. Grease and flour two 7x3 inch loaf pans. Preheat oven to 350 degrees F (175 degrees C).
2. In one bowl, whisk together flour, soda, salt, and sugar. Mix in slightly beaten eggs, melted butter, and mashed bananas. Stir in nuts if desired. Pour into prepared pans.
3. Bake at 350 degrees F (175 degrees C) for 1 hour, or until a wooden toothpick inserted in the center comes out clean.

FRENCH TOAST CASSEROLE

Servings: 6 | Prep: 30m | Cooks: 50m | Total: 1h20m

NUTRITION FACTS

Calories: 207 | Carbohydrates: 26.6g | Fat: 7.2g | Protein: 8.5g | Cholesterol: 129mg

INGREDIENTS

- 5 cups bread cubes
- 1/4 teaspoon salt
- 4 eggs
- 1 teaspoon vanilla extract
- 1 1/2 cups milk
- 1 tablespoon margarine, softened
- 1/4 cup white sugar, divided
- 1 teaspoon ground cinnamon

DIRECTIONS

1. Preheat oven to 350 degrees F (175 degrees C). Lightly butter an 8x8 inch baking pan.
2. Line bottom of pan with bread cubes. In a large bowl, beat together eggs, milk, 2 tablespoons sugar, salt and vanilla. pour egg mixture over bread. Dot with margarine; let stand for 10 minutes.
3. Combine remaining 2 tablespoons sugar with 1 teaspoon cinnamon and sprinkle over the top. Bake in preheated oven about 45 to 50 minutes, until top is golden.

EASY PANCAKES

Servings: 4 | Prep: 5m | Cooks: 10m | Total: 15m

NUTRITION FACTS

Calories: 247 | Carbohydrates: 33.5g | Fat: 9.6g | Protein: 6.8g | Cholesterol: 51mg

INGREDIENTS

- 1 cup all-purpose flour
- 1 egg, beaten
- 2 tablespoons white sugar
- 1 cup milk
- 2 teaspoons baking powder
- 2 tablespoons vegetable oil
- 1 teaspoon salt

DIRECTIONS

1. In a large bowl, mix flour, sugar, baking powder and salt. Make a well in the center, and pour in milk, egg and oil. Mix until smooth.
2. Heat a lightly oiled griddle or frying pan over medium high heat. Pour or scoop the batter onto the griddle, using approximately 1/4 cup for each pancake. Brown on both sides and serve hot.

QUICK QUICHE

Servings: 6 | Prep: 15m | Cooks: 35m | Total: 50m

NUTRITION FACTS

Calories: 291 | Carbohydrates: 12.9g | Fat: 18.8g | Protein: 17g | Cholesterol: 170mg

INGREDIENTS

- 8 slices bacon
- 1/4 cup finely chopped onion
- 4 ounces shredded Swiss cheese
- 1 teaspoon salt
- 2 tablespoons butter, melted
- 1/2 cup all-purpose flour
- 4 eggs, beaten
- 1 1/2 cups milk

DIRECTIONS

1. Place bacon in a large, deep skillet. Cook over medium high heat until evenly brown. Drain, crumble and set aside.
2. Preheat oven to 350 degrees F (175 degrees C). Lightly grease a 9 inch pie pan.
3. Line bottom of pie plate with cheese and crumbled bacon. Combine eggs, butter, onion, salt, flour and milk; whisk together until smooth; pour into pie pan.
4. Bake in preheated oven for 35 minutes, until set. Serve hot or cold.

EASY BROCCOLI QUICHE

Servings: 6 | Prep: 20m | Cooks: 30m | Total: 50m

NUTRITION FACTS

Calories: 388 | Carbohydrates: 21.5g | Fat: 26.8g | Protein: 16.1g | Cholesterol: 167mg

INGREDIENTS

- 1 (9 inch) unbaked pie crust
- 4 eggs, well beaten
- 3 tablespoons butter, divided
- 1 1/2 cups milk
- 1 onion, minced
- 1 teaspoon salt
- 1 teaspoon minced garlic
- 1/2 teaspoon black pepper
- 2 cups chopped fresh broccoli
- 1 tablespoon butter, melted

- 1 1/2 cups shredded mozzarella cheese

DIRECTIONS

1. Preheat oven to 350 degrees F (175 degrees C). Line a 9-inch deep-dish pie pan with crust.
2. Melt 2 tablespoons butter in a large saucepan over medium-low heat. Add onion, garlic, and broccoli. Cook slowly, stirring occasionally, until vegetables are soft. Spoon vegetables into crust and sprinkle with cheese.
3. Combine eggs and milk. Season with salt and pepper. Stir in remaining 1 tablespoon melted butter. Pour egg mixture over vegetables and cheese.
4. Bake in preheated oven until center has set, 30 to 50 minutes.

IRRESISTIBLE IRISH SODA BREAD

Servings: 12 | Prep: 15m | Cooks: 1h10m | Total: 1h25m

NUTRITION FACTS

Calories: 192 | Carbohydrates: 31.7g | Fat: 4.9g | Protein: 5.1g | Cholesterol: 27mg

INGREDIENTS

- 3 cups all-purpose flour
- 1 teaspoon baking soda
- 1 tablespoon baking powder
- 1 egg, lightly beaten
- 1/3 cup white sugar
- 2 cups buttermilk
- 1 teaspoon salt
- 1/4 cup butter, melted

DIRECTIONS

1. Preheat oven to 325 degrees F (165 degrees C). Grease a 9x5 inch loaf pan.
2. Combine flour, baking powder, sugar, salt and baking soda. Blend egg and buttermilk together, and add all at once to the flour mixture. Mix just until moistened. Stir in butter. Pour into prepared pan.
3. Bake for 65 to 70 minutes, or until a toothpick inserted in the bread comes out clean. Cool on a wire rack. Wrap in foil for several hours, or overnight, for best flavor.

TODD'S FAMOUS BLUEBERRY PANCAKES

Servings: 6 | Prep: 10m | Cooks: 15m | Total: 1h15m

NUTRITION FACTS

Calories: 146 | Carbohydrates: 24.7g | Fat: 2.9g | Protein: 5.1g | Cholesterol: 37mg

INGREDIENTS

- 1 1/4 cups all-purpose flour
- 1 egg
- 1/2 teaspoon salt
- 1 cup milk
- 1 tablespoon baking powder
- 1/2 tablespoon butter, melted
- 1 1/4 teaspoons white sugar
- 1/2 cup frozen blueberries, thawed

DIRECTIONS

1. In a large bowl, sift together flour, salt, baking powder and sugar. In a small bowl, beat together egg and milk. Stir milk and egg into flour mixture. Mix in the butter and fold in the blueberries. Set aside for 1 hour.
2. Heat a lightly oiled griddle or frying pan over medium high heat. Pour or scoop the batter onto the griddle, using approximately 1/4 cup for each pancake. Brown on both sides and serve hot.

MEGAN'S GRANOLA

Servings: 30 | Prep: 20m | Cooks: 20m | Total: 40m

NUTRITION FACTS

Calories: 369 | Carbohydrates: 45g | Fat: 20g | Protein: 8.3g | Cholesterol: 0mg

INGREDIENTS

- 8 cups rolled oats
- 1/2 cup brown sugar
- 1 1/2 cups wheat germ
- 1/4 cup maple syrup
- 1 1/2 cups oat bran
- 3/4 cup honey
- 1 cup sunflower seeds
- 1 cup vegetable oil
- 1 cup finely chopped almonds
- 1 tablespoon ground cinnamon
- 1 cup finely chopped pecans
- 1 tablespoon vanilla extract

- 1 cup finely chopped walnuts
- 2 cups raisins or sweetened dried cranberries
- 1 1/2 teaspoons salt

DIRECTIONS

1. Preheat the oven to 325 degrees F (165 degrees C). Line two large baking sheets with parchment or aluminum foil.
2. Combine the oats, wheat germ, oat bran, sunflower seeds, almonds, pecans, and walnuts in a large bowl. Stir together the salt, brown sugar, maple syrup, honey, oil, cinnamon, and vanilla in a saucepan. Bring to a boil over medium heat, then pour over the dry ingredients, and stir to coat. Spread the mixture out evenly on the baking sheets.
3. Bake in the preheated oven until crispy and toasted, about 20 minutes. Stir once halfway through. Cool, then stir in the raisins or cranberries before storing in an airtight container.

CATHY'S BANANA BREAD

Servings: 16 | Prep: 10m | Cooks: 50m | Total: 1hm

NUTRITION FACTS

Calories: 200 | Carbohydrates: 32.6g | Fat: 6.6g | Protein: 3g | Cholesterol: 30mg

INGREDIENTS

- 1 cup mashed bananas
- 1 teaspoon vanilla extract
- 1 cup sour cream
- 2 cups all-purpose flour
- 1/4 cup margarine
- 1 teaspoon baking soda
- 1 1/3 cups white sugar
- 1 teaspoon baking powder
- 2 eggs
- 1/4 teaspoon salt

DIRECTIONS

1. Preheat oven to 350 degrees F (175 degrees C). Grease and flour one 9x13 inch pan, or two 7x3 inch loaf pans.
2. Combine banana and sour cream. Set aside. In a large bowl, cream together the margarine and sugar until smooth. Beat in the eggs one at a time, then stir in the vanilla and banana mixture. Combine the flour, baking soda, baking powder and salt; stir into the banana mixture. Spread the batter evenly into the prepared pan or pans.

3. Bake for 50 minutes in the preheated oven, or until a toothpick inserted into the center of the bread comes out clean.

PANCAKESS

Servings: 3 | Prep: 5m | Cooks: 10m | Total: 20m

NUTRITION FACTS

Calories: 315 | Carbohydrates: 40.2g | Fat: 13g | Protein: 9.1g | Cholesterol: 69mg

INGREDIENTS

- 1 cup all-purpose flour
- 1/4 teaspoon salt
- 1 tablespoon white sugar
- 1 cup milk
- 1 teaspoon baking powder
- 1 egg
- 1/2 teaspoon baking soda
- 2 tablespoons vegetable oil

DIRECTIONS

1. Preheat a lightly oiled griddle over medium-high heat.
2. Combine flour, sugar, baking powder, baking soda and salt. Make a well in the center. In a separate bowl, beat together egg, milk and oil. Pour milk mixture into flour mixture. Beat until smooth.
3. Pour or scoop the batter onto the hot griddle, using approximately 1/4 cup for each pancake. Brown on both sides and serve hot.

SAUSAGE CASSEROLE

Servings: 12 | Prep: 25m | Cooks: 1h15m | Total: 1h45m | Additional: 5m

NUTRITION FACTS

Calories: 355 | Carbohydrates: 7.9g | Fat: 26.3g | Protein: 21.6g | Cholesterol: 188mg

INGREDIENTS

- 1 pound sage flavored breakfast sausage
- 1/2 cup onion, shredded
- 3 cups shredded potatoes, drained and pressed
- 1 (16 ounce) container small curd cottage cheese
- 1/4 cup butter, melted

- 6 jumbo eggs
- 12 ounces mild Cheddar cheese, shredded

DIRECTIONS

1. Preheat oven to 375 degrees F (190 degrees C). Lightly grease a 9x13 inch square baking dish.
2. Place sausage in a large, deep skillet. Cook over medium-high heat until evenly brown. Drain, crumble, and set aside.
3. In the prepared baking dish, stir together the shredded potatoes and butter. Line the bottom and sides of the baking dish with the mixture. In a bowl, mix the sausage, Cheddar cheese, onion, cottage cheese, and eggs. Pour over the potato mixture.
4. Bake 1 hour in the preheated oven, or until a toothpick inserted into center of the casserole comes out clean. Let cool for 5 minutes before serving.

SAUSAGE BALLS

Servings: 15 | Prep: 15m | Cooks: 20m | Total: 35m

NUTRITION FACTS

Calories: 264 | Carbohydrates: 10.5g | Fat: 19g | Protein: 12.8g | Cholesterol: 49mg

INGREDIENTS

- 1 pound ground pork sausage
- 1 pound sharp Cheddar cheese, shredded
- 2 cups biscuit baking mix

DIRECTIONS

1. Preheat oven to 350 degrees F (175 degrees C).
2. In a large bowl, combine sausage, biscuit baking mix and cheese. Form into walnut size balls and place on baking sheets.
3. Bake in preheated oven for 20 to 25 minutes, until golden brown and sausage is cooked through.

CINNAMON BREAD

Servings: 12 | Prep: 20m | Cooks: 50m | Total: 1h10m

NUTRITION FACTS

Calories: 218 | Carbohydrates: 36.4g | Fat: 6.4g | Protein: 3.9g | Cholesterol: 32mg

INGREDIENTS

- 2 cups all-purpose flour
- 1/4 cup vegetable oil
- 1 cup white sugar
- 2 eggs
- 2 teaspoons baking powder
- 2 teaspoons vanilla extract
- 1/2 teaspoon baking soda
- 2 tablespoons white sugar
- 1 1/2 teaspoons ground cinnamon
- 1 teaspoon ground cinnamon
- 1 teaspoon salt
- 2 teaspoons margarine
- 1 cup buttermilk

DIRECTIONS

1. Preheat oven to 350 degrees F (175 degrees C). Grease one 9x5 inch loaf pan.
2. Measure flour, 1 cup sugar, baking powder, baking soda, 1 1/2 teaspoons cinnamon, salt, buttermilk, oil, eggs and vanilla into large mixing bowl. Beat 3 minutes. Pour into prepared loaf pan. Smooth top.
3. Combine 2 tablespoons white sugar, 1 teaspoon cinnamon and butter, mixing until crumbly. Sprinkle topping over smoothed batter. Using knife, cut in a light swirling motion to give a marbled effect.
4. Bake for about 50 minutes. Test with toothpick. When inserted it should come out clean. Remove bread from pan to rack to cool.

ZUCCHINI BREAD

Servings: 24 | Prep: 15m | Cooks: 1h10m | Total: 1h25m

NUTRITION FACTS

Calories: 231 | Carbohydrates: 29.6g | Fat: 11.6g | Protein: 2.9g | Cholesterol: 23mg

INGREDIENTS

- 3 eggs
- 3 teaspoons ground cinnamon
- 1 cup vegetable oil
- 1 teaspoon baking soda
- 2 cups white sugar
- 1/4 teaspoon baking powder
- 2 cups grated zucchini
- 1 teaspoon salt

- 2 teaspoons vanilla extract
- 1/2 cup chopped walnuts
- 3 cups all-purpose flour

DIRECTIONS

1. Preheat oven to 325 degrees F (165 degrees C). Grease and flour two 8x4 inch loaf pans.
2. In a large bowl, beat eggs until light and frothy. Mix in oil and sugar. Stir in zucchini and vanilla. Combine flour, cinnamon, soda, baking powder, salt and nuts; stir into the egg mixture. Divide batter into prepared pans.
3. Bake for 60 to 70 minutes, or until done.

CREPES

Servings: 8 | Prep: 5m | Cooks: 15m | Total: 1h20m

NUTRITION FACTS

Calories: 79 | Carbohydrates: 9.5g | Fat: 2.8g | Protein: 3.7g | Cholesterol: 49mg

INGREDIENTS

- 2 eggs
- 1 pinch salt
- 1 cup milk
- 1 1/2 teaspoons vegetable oil
- 2/3 cup all-purpose flour

DIRECTIONS

1. In a blender combine eggs, milk, flour, salt and oil. Process until smooth. Cover and refrigerate 1 hour.
2. Heat a skillet over medium-high heat and brush with oil. Pour 1/4 cup of crepe batter into pan, tilting to completely coat the surface of the pan. Cook 2 to 5 minutes, turning once, until golden. Repeat with remaining batter.

DESSERT CREPES

Servings: 8 | Prep: 10m | Cooks: 10m | Total: 20m

NUTRITION FACTS

Calories: 164 | Carbohydrates: 17.2g | Fat: 7.7g | Protein: 6.4g | Cholesterol: 111mg

INGREDIENTS

- 4 eggs, lightly beaten
- 1 cup all-purpose flour
- 1 1/3 cups milk
- 2 tablespoons white sugar
- 2 tablespoons butter, melted
- 1/2 teaspoon salt

DIRECTIONS

1. In large bowl, whisk together eggs, milk, melted butter, flour sugar and salt until smooth.
2. Heat a medium-sized skillet or crepe pan over medium heat. Grease pan with a small amount of butter or oil applied with a brush or paper towel. Using a serving spoon or small ladle, spoon about 3 tablespoons crepe batter into hot pan, tilting the pan so that bottom surface is evenly coated. Cook over medium heat, 1 to 2 minutes on a side, or until golden brown. Serve immediately.

MOM'S BUTTERMILK PANCAKES

Servings: 4 | Prep: 15m | Cooks: 15m | Total: 30m

NUTRITION FACTS

Calories: 210 | Carbohydrates: 27.2g | Fat: 7.9g | Protein: 7.1g | Cholesterol: 65mg

INGREDIENTS

- 1 cup flour
- 1 egg
- 1 teaspoon salt
- 1 1/8 cups buttermilk
- 1 teaspoon baking soda
- 2 tablespoons butter, melted

DIRECTIONS

1. Preheat and lightly grease a large skillet or electric griddle.
2. Mix the flour, salt, and baking soda together in a bowl. Add the egg, buttermilk, and butter; stir together lightly, but keep it lumpy. The batter should look thick, spongy, and puffy.
3. Drop 1/3 cup of the batter onto the cooking surface, spreading lightly with the bottom of the cup. Cook until lightly-browned on each side, 1 to 2 minutes per side.

TRUCK-STOP BUTTERMILK PANCAKES

Servings: 12 | Prep: 10m | Cooks: 5m | Total: 15m

NUTRITION FACTS

Calories: 347 | Carbohydrates: 51.8g | Fat: 9.8g | Protein: 12.4g | Cholesterol: 99mg

INGREDIENTS

- 5 eggs
- 5 teaspoons baking powder
- 1 1/2 cups milk
- 5 teaspoons baking soda
- 6 tablespoons butter, melted
- 1 pinch salt (optional)
- 5 cups buttermilk
- 5 tablespoons sugar
- 5 cups all-purpose flour

DIRECTIONS

1. In a large bowl, whisk together the eggs, milk, butter and buttermilk. Combine the flour, baking powder, baking soda and sugar; stir into the wet ingredients just until blended. Adjust the thickness of the batter to your liking by adding more flour or buttermilk if necessary.
2. Heat a large skillet over medium heat, and coat with cooking spray. Pour 1/4 cupfuls of batter onto the skillet, and cook until bubbles appear on the surface. Flip with a spatula, and cook until browned on the other side. Continue with remaining batter.

CREME BRULEE FRENCH TOAST

Servings: 6 | Prep: 20m | Cooks: 40m | Total: 9h

NUTRITION FACTS

Calories: 510 | Carbohydrates: 58.7g | Fat: 26.9g | Protein: 10.2g | Cholesterol: 218mg

INGREDIENTS

- 1/2 cup unsalted butter
- 1 1/2 cups half-and-half cream
- 1 cup packed brown sugar
- 1 teaspoon vanilla extract
- 2 tablespoons corn syrup
- 1 teaspoon brandy-based orange liqueur (such as Grand Marnier)
- 6 (1-inch thick) slices French bread
- 1/4 teaspoon salt
- 5 eggs

DIRECTIONS

1. Melt butter in a small saucepan over medium heat. Mix in brown sugar and corn syrup, stirring until sugar is dissolved. Pour into a 9x13 inch baking dish.
2. Remove crusts from bread, and arrange in the baking dish in a single layer. In a small bowl, whisk together eggs, half and half, vanilla extract, orange brandy, and salt. Pour over the bread. Cover, and chill at least 8 hours, or overnight.
3. Preheat oven to 350 degrees F (175 degrees C). Remove the dish from the refrigerator, and bring to room temperature.
4. Bake uncovered 35 to 40 minutes in the preheated oven, until puffed and lightly browned.

OLD CHARLESTON STYLE SHRIMP AND GRITS

Servings: 8 | Prep: 30m | Cooks: 45m | Total: 1h15m

NUTRITION FACTS

Calories: 618 | Carbohydrates: 16.2g | Fat: 43.7g | Protein: 38.6g | Cholesterol: 270mg

INGREDIENTS

- 1 cup coarsely ground grits
- 1 green bell pepper, chopped
- 3 cups water
- 1 red bell pepper, chopped
- 2 teaspoons salt
- 1 yellow bell pepper, chopped
- 2 cups half-and-half
- 1 cup chopped onion
- 2 pounds uncooked shrimp, peeled and deveined
- 1 teaspoon minced garlic
- salt to taste
- 1/4 cup butter
- 1 pinch cayenne pepper, or to taste
- 1/4 cup all-purpose flour
- 1 lemon, juiced
- 1 cup chicken broth
- 1 pound andouille sausage, cut into 1/4-inch slices
- 1 tablespoon Worcestershire sauce
- 5 slices bacon
- 1 cup shredded sharp Cheddar cheese

DIRECTIONS

1. Bring water, grits, and salt to a boil in a heavy saucepan with a lid. Stir in half-and-half and simmer until grits are thickened and tender, 15 to 20 minutes. Set aside and keep warm.

2. Sprinkle shrimp with salt and cayenne pepper; drizzle with lemon juice. Set aside in a bowl.
3. Place andouille sausage slices in a large skillet over medium heat; fry sausage until browned, 5 to 8 minutes. Remove skillet from heat.
4. Cook bacon in a large skillet over medium-high heat, turning occasionally, until evenly browned, about 10 minutes. Retain bacon drippings in skillet. Transfer bacon slices to paper towels, let cool, and crumble.
5. Cook and stir green, red, and yellow bell peppers, onion, and garlic in the bacon drippings until the onion is translucent, about 8 minutes.
6. Stir shrimp and cooked vegetables into the andouille sausage and mix to combine.
7. Melt butter in a saucepan over medium heat; stir in flour to make a smooth paste. Turn heat to low and cook, stirring constantly, until the mixture is medium brown in color, 8 to 10 minutes. Watch carefully, mixture burns easily.
8. Pour the butter-flour mixture into the skillet with andouille sausage, shrimp, and vegetables. Place the skillet over medium heat and pour in chicken broth, bacon and Worcestershire sauce, cooking and stirring until the sauce thickens and the shrimp become opaque and bright pink, about 8 minutes.
9. Just before serving, mix sharp Cheddar cheese into grits until melted and grits are creamy and light yellow. Serve shrimp mixture over cheese grits.

OLD-FASHIONED PANCAKES
Servings: 4 | Prep: 5m | Cooks: 20m | Total: 25m

NUTRITION FACTS

Calories: 318 | Carbohydrates: 43.7g | Fat: 11.9g | Protein: 9g | Cholesterol: 75mg

INGREDIENTS

- 1 1/2 cups all-purpose flour
- 3 tablespoons butter, melted
- 3 1/2 teaspoons baking powder
- 1 egg
- 1 teaspoon salt
- 1 1/4 cups milk
- 1 tablespoon white sugar
- cooking spray

DIRECTIONS

1. Sift together flour, baking powder, salt, and sugar in a large bowl.
2. Whisk in melted butter, egg, and milk until combined. Let batter rest for 5 minutes.

3. Preheat a large skillet over medium-high heat. Spray with cooking spray. Pour batter into the hot skillet, about 1/4 cup of batter for each pancake. Cook for 2 to 3 minutes, until bubbles appear on the sides and center of each pancake. Flip and cook until golden, about 1 to 2 minutes.

OATMEAL PANCAKES
Servings: 4 | Prep: 10m | Cooks: 10m | Total: 20m

NUTRITION FACTS

Calories: 207 | Carbohydrates: 24.6g | Fat: 9.3g | Protein: 6g | Cholesterol: 48mg

INGREDIENTS

- 1/2 cup all-purpose flour
- 1/2 teaspoon salt
- 1/2 cup quick cooking oats
- 3/4 cup buttermilk
- 1 tablespoon white sugar
- 1 teaspoon vanilla extract
- 1 teaspoon baking powder
- 2 tablespoons vegetable oil
- 1/2 teaspoon baking soda
- 1 egg

DIRECTIONS

1. Place flour, oats, sugar, baking powder, baking soda, salt, buttermilk, vanilla, oil and egg in a food processor and puree until smooth.
2. Heat a lightly oiled griddle or frying pan over medium high heat. Pour or scoop the batter onto the griddle, using approximately 1/4 cup for each pancake. Brown on both sides and serve hot.

EASY QUICHE
Servings: 8 | Prep: 10m | Cooks: 50m | Total: 1h

NUTRITION FACTS

Calories: 371 | Carbohydrates: 12.5g | Fat: 26.6g | Protein: 21g | Cholesterol: 161mg

INGREDIENTS

- 2 cups milk
- 1 cup grated Parmesan cheese
- 4 eggs

- 1 (10 ounce) package chopped frozen broccoli, thawed and drained
- 3/4 cup biscuit baking mix
- 1 cup cubed cooked ham
- 1/4 cup butter, softened
- 8 ounces shredded Cheddar cheese

DIRECTIONS

1. Preheat oven to 375 degrees F (190 degrees C). Lightly grease a 10 inch quiche dish.
2. In a large bowl, beat together milk, eggs, baking mix, butter and parmesan cheese. Batter will be lumpy. Stir in broccoli, ham and Cheddar cheese. Pour into prepared quiche dish.
3. Bake in preheated oven for 50 minutes, until eggs are set and top is golden brown.

EGG AND SAUSAGE CASSEROLE

Servings: 12 | Prep: 15m | Cooks: 35m | Total: 50m

NUTRITION FACTS

Calories: 341 | Carbohydrates: 8.7g | Fat: 24.7g | Protein: 19.9g | Cholesterol: 177mg

INGREDIENTS

- 1 pound pork sausage
- 2 cups shredded mozzarella cheese
- 1 (8 ounce) package refrigerated crescent roll dough
- 2 cups shredded Cheddar cheese
- 8 eggs, beaten
- 1 teaspoon dried oregano

DIRECTIONS

1. Place sausage in a large, deep skillet. Cook over medium-high heat until evenly brown. Drain, crumble, and set aside.
2. Preheat oven to 325 degrees F (165 degrees C). Lightly grease a 9x13 inch baking dish.
3. Line the bottom of the prepared baking dish with crescent roll dough, and sprinkle with crumbled sausage. In a large bowl, mix beaten eggs, mozzarella, and Cheddar. Season the mixture with oregano, and pour over the sausage and crescent rolls.
4. Bake 25 to 30 minutes in the preheated oven, or until a knife inserted in the center comes out clean.

PANCAKES

Servings: 4 | Prep: 10m | Cooks: 10m | Total: 20m

NUTRITION FACTS

Calories: 263 | Carbohydrates: 40.3g | Fat: 8.4g | Protein: 6.8g | Cholesterol: 51mg

INGREDIENTS

- 1 cup all-purpose flour
- 1 cup milk, at room temperature
- 1/4 cup white sugar
- 1 egg, at room temperature
- 1 tablespoon baking powder
- 1 tablespoon oil
- 1/4 teaspoon salt
- 2 teaspoons oil, or as needed

DIRECTIONS

1. Combine flour, sugar, baking powder, and salt in a bowl; make a 'well' in the center of the flour mixture. Pour milk, eggs, and 1 tablespoon oil into the well. Mix until well moistened.
2. Place a griddle over medium-high heat; sprinkle a few drops of water onto the griddle. If the droplets bounce, the griddle is ready; add 2 teaspoons oil.
3. Spoon batter onto the griddle; cook until bubbles form and the edges are dry, 3 to 5 minutes. Flip and cook until browned on the other side, 3 to 5 more minutes. Repeat with remaining batter.

BAKED OATMEAL

Servings: 8 | Prep: 10m | Cooks: 40m | Total: 50m

NUTRITION FACTS

Calories: 393 | Carbohydrates: 59.2g | Fat: 15.3g | Protein: 6.8g | Cholesterol: 79mg

INGREDIENTS

- 3 cups rolled oats
- 1 cup milk
- 1 cup brown sugar
- 2 eggs
- 2 teaspoons ground cinnamon
- 1/2 cup melted butter
- 2 teaspoons baking powder
- 2 teaspoons vanilla extract
- 1 teaspoon salt
- 3/4 cup dried cranberries

DIRECTIONS

1. Preheat oven to 350 degrees F (175 degrees C).
2. In a large bowl, mix together oats, brown sugar, cinnamon, baking powder, and salt. Beat in milk, eggs, melted butter, and vanilla extract. Stir in dried cranberries. Spread into a 9x13 inch baking dish.
3. Bake in preheated oven for 40 minutes.

EASY SAUSAGE GRAVY AND BISCUITS
Servings: 8 | Prep: 5m | Cooks: 10m | Total: 15m

NUTRITION FACTS

Calories: 333 | Carbohydrates: 30.8g | Fat: 18.7g | Protein: 9.8g | Cholesterol: 25mg

INGREDIENTS

- 1 (16 ounce) can refrigerated jumbo buttermilk biscuits
- 2 1/2 cups milk
- 1 (9.6 ounce) package Jimmy Dean Original Hearty Pork Sausage Crumbles
- Salt and ground black pepper to taste
- 1/4 cup flour

DIRECTIONS

1. Bake biscuits according to package directions.
2. Meanwhile, cook sausage in large skillet over medium heat 5-6 minutes or until thoroughly heated, stirring frequently. Stir in flour. Gradually add milk; cook until mixture comes to a boil and thickens, stirring constantly. Reduce heat to medium-low; simmer 2 minutes, stirring constantly. Season to taste with salt and pepper.
3. Split biscuits in half. Place 2 halves on each of 8 plates; top with about 1/3 cup gravy.

WHOLE GRAIN WAFFLES
Servings: 6 | Prep: 10m | Cooks: 5m | Total: 15m

NUTRITION FACTS

Calories: 288 | Carbohydrates: 28.4g | Fat: 15.8g | Protein: 9.9g | Cholesterol: 63mg

INGREDIENTS

- 2 eggs, beaten
- 1/2 cup flax seed meal
- 1 3/4 cups skim milk
- 1/4 cup wheat germ

- 1/4 cup canola oil
- 1/4 cup all-purpose flour
- 1/4 cup unsweetened applesauce
- 4 teaspoons baking powder
- 1 teaspoon vanilla extract
- 1 tablespoon sugar
- 1 cup whole wheat pastry flour
- 1/4 teaspoon salt

DIRECTIONS

1. In a large bowl, whisk together the eggs, milk, oil, applesauce, and vanilla. Beat in whole wheat pastry flour, flax seed meal, wheat germ, all-purpose flour, baking powder, sugar, and salt until batter is smooth.
2. Preheat a waffle iron, and coat with cooking spray. Pour batter into waffle iron in batches, and cook until crisp and golden brown.

VANILLA CREPES

Servings: 12 | Prep: 10m | Cooks: 20m | Total: 30m

NUTRITION FACTS

Calories: 142 | Carbohydrates: 15.9g | Fat: 6.7g | Protein: 3.3g | Cholesterol: 66mg

INGREDIENTS

- 1 1/2 cups milk
- 2 tablespoons sugar
- 3 egg yolks
- 1/2 teaspoon salt
- 2 tablespoons vanilla extract
- 5 tablespoons melted butter
- 1 1/2 cups all-purpose flour

DIRECTIONS

1. In a large bowl, mix together the milk, egg yolks and vanilla. Stir in the flour, sugar, salt and melted butter until well blended.
2. Heat a crepe pan over medium heat until hot. Coat with vegetable oil or cooking spray. Pour about 1/4 cup of batter into the pan and tip to spread the batter to the edges. When bubbles form on the top and the edges are dry, flip over and cook until lightly browned on the other side and edges are golden. Repeat with remaining batter.
3. Fill crepes with your favorite fruit, cream, caramel or even ice cream or cheese to serve.

GERMAN POTATO PANCAKES

Servings: 6 | Prep: 25m | Cooks: 6m | Total: 45m | Additional: 14m

NUTRITION FACTS

Calories: 283 | Carbohydrates: 40.7g | Fat: 11g | Protein: 6.8g | Cholesterol: 62mg

INGREDIENTS

- 2 eggs
- 1/4 teaspoon pepper
- 2 tablespoons all-purpose flour
- 6 medium potatoes, peeled and shredded
- 1/4 teaspoon baking powder
- 1/2 cup finely chopped onion
- 1/2 teaspoon salt
- 1/4 cup vegetable oil

DIRECTIONS

1. In a large bowl, beat together eggs, flour, baking powder, salt, and pepper. Mix in potatoes and onion.
2. Heat oil in a large skillet over medium heat. In batches, drop heaping tablespoonfuls of the potato mixture into the skillet. Press to flatten. Cook about 3 minutes on each side, until browned and crisp. Drain on paper towels.

VEGAN PANCAKES

Servings: 3 | Prep: 5m | Cooks: 10m | Total: 15m

NUTRITION FACTS

Calories: 264 | Carbohydrates: 48.9g | Fat: 5.1g | Protein: 5.4g | Cholesterol: 0mg

INGREDIENTS

- 1 1/4 cups all-purpose flour
- 1/2 teaspoon salt
- 2 tablespoons white sugar
- 1 1/4 cups water
- 2 teaspoons baking powder
- 1 tablespoon oil

DIRECTIONS

1. Sift the flour, sugar, baking powder, and salt into a large bowl. Whisk the water and oil together in a small bowl. Make a well in the center of the dry ingredients, and pour in the wet. Stir just until blended; mixture will be lumpy.
2. Heat a lightly oiled griddle over medium-high heat. Drop batter by large spoonfuls onto the griddle, and cook until bubbles form and the edges are dry. Flip, and cook until browned on the other side. Repeat with remaining batter.

BACON FOR THE FAMILY OR A CROWD

Servings: 4 | Prep: 5m | Cooks: 15m | Total: 20m

NUTRITION FACTS

Calories: 203 | Carbohydrates: 0.5g | Fat: 15.6g | Protein: 13.9g | Cholesterol: 41mg

INGREDIENTS

- 1 pound thick sliced bacon

DIRECTIONS

1. Preheat oven to 350 degrees F (175 degrees C). Line a baking sheet with aluminum foil. Arrange bacon on baking sheet in a single layer with the edges touching or slightly overlapping.
2. Bake in preheated oven to desired degree of doneness, 10 to 15 minutes. Remove bacon from the baking sheet with tongs or a fork, and drain on a paper towel-lined plate.

BAKED HAM AND CHEESE PARTY SANDWICHES

Servings: 24 | Prep: 15m | Cooks: 20m | Total: 35m

NUTRITION FACTS

Calories: 208 | Carbohydrates: 10.8g | Fat: 14g | Protein: 9.8g | Cholesterol: 43mg

INGREDIENTS

- 3/4 cup melted butter
- 1 tablespoon dried minced onion
- 1 1/2 tablespoons Dijon mustard
- 24 mini sandwich rolls
- 1 1/2 teaspoons Worcestershire sauce
- 1 pound thinly sliced cooked deli ham
- 1 1/2 tablespoons poppy seeds
- 1 pound thinly sliced Swiss cheese

DIRECTIONS

1. Preheat oven to 350 degrees F (175 degrees C). Grease a 9x13-inch baking dish.
2. In a bowl, mix together butter, Dijon mustard, Worcestershire sauce, poppy seeds, and dried onion. Separate the tops from bottoms of the rolls, and place the bottom pieces into the prepared baking dish. Layer about half the ham onto the rolls. Arrange the Swiss cheese over the ham, and top with remaining ham slices in a layer. Place the tops of the rolls onto the sandwiches. Pour the mustard mixture evenly over the rolls.
3. Bake in the preheated oven until the rolls are lightly browned and the cheese has melted, about 20 minutes. Slice into individual rolls through the ham and cheese layers to serve.

UGLIES
Servings: 8 | Prep: 20m | Cooks: 15m | Total: 40m

NUTRITION FACTS

Calories: 360 | Carbohydrates: 33.6g | Fat: 17.2g | Protein: 17.2g | Cholesterol: 56mg

INGREDIENTS

- 1 pound ground beef chuck
- 1 1/2 cups barbeque sauce
- 1/2 cup chopped onion
- 1 (10 ounce) package refrigerated biscuit dough
- 1/2 teaspoon garlic powder
- 2 cups shredded Cheddar cheese

DIRECTIONS

1. Preheat oven to 400 degrees F (200 degrees C). Lightly grease 8 muffin cups.
2. In a large skillet or frying pan, cook ground chuck with onion and garlic powder until evenly brown; drain off the grease. Stir in the barbeque sauce and simmer for another 3 minutes.
3. Roll out each biscuit on a floured surface so that each biscuit is 6 inches across. Put the biscuit in the muffin tin and fold up sides to create a cup shape. Fill each biscuit fill almost to the top with the meat mixture; top with cheddar cheese.
4. Bake in preheated oven until biscuits are baked, cheese is melted and tops are golden brown, about 15 minutes.

LIGHT AND FLUFFY SPINACH QUICHE
Servings: 6 | Prep: 20m | Cooks: 1h | Total: 1h20m

NUTRITION FACTS

Calories: 356 | Carbohydrates: 19.9g | Fat: 23.2g | Protein: 17.9g | Cholesterol: 141mg

INGREDIENTS

- 1/2 cup light mayonnaise
- 1 (10 ounce) package frozen chopped spinach, thawed and squeezed dry
- 1/2 cup milk
- 1/4 cup chopped onion
- 4 eggs, lightly beaten
- 1 (9 inch) unbaked pie shell
- 8 ounces shredded reduced-fat Cheddar cheese

DIRECTIONS

1. Preheat oven to 400 degrees F (200 degrees C). Line a cookie sheet with foil.
2. In a large bowl, whisk together mayonnaise and milk until smooth. Whisk in eggs. Layer spinach, cheese, and onion in pie shell, making several layers of each. Pour in egg mixture. Place quiche on prepared cookie sheet. Cover quiche with foil.
3. Bake in preheated oven for 45 minutes. Remove cover, and bake 10 to 15 minutes, or until top is golden brown and filling is set.

WHOLE WHEAT BLUEBERRY PANCAKES

Servings: 5 | Prep: 5m | Cooks: 8m | Total: 13m

NUTRITION FACTS

Calories: 160 | Carbohydrates: 26.7g | Fat: 2.6g | Protein: 9.8g | Cholesterol: 41mg

INGREDIENTS

- 1 1/4 cups whole wheat flour
- 1/2 teaspoon salt
- 2 teaspoons baking powder
- 1 tablespoon artificial sweetener
- 1 egg
- 1/2 cup blueberries
- 1 cup milk, plus more if necessary

DIRECTIONS

1. Sift together flour and baking powder, set aside. Beat together the egg, milk, salt and artificial sweetener in a bowl. Stir in flour until just moistened, add blueberries, and stir to incorporate.

2. Preheat a heavy-bottomed skillet over medium heat, and spray with cooking spray. Pour approximately 1/4 cup of the batter into the pan for each pancake. Cook until bubbly, about 1 1/2 minutes. Turn, and continue cooking until golden brown.

BREAKFAST PIES

Servings: 10 | Prep: 20m | Cooks: 20m | Total: 40m

NUTRITION FACTS

Calories: 247 | Carbohydrates: 15.8g | Fat: 15.7g | Protein: 10.5g | Cholesterol: 82mg

INGREDIENTS

- 3/4 pound breakfast sausage
- 3 eggs, beaten
- 1/8 cup minced onion
- 3 tablespoons milk
- 1/8 cup minced green bell pepper
- 1/2 cup shredded Colby-Monterey Jack cheese
- 1 (12 ounce) can refrigerated biscuit dough

DIRECTIONS

1. Preheat oven to 400 degrees F (200 degrees C).
2. In a large, deep skillet over medium-high heat, combine sausage, onion and green pepper. Cook until sausage is evenly brown. Drain, crumble, and set aside.
3. Separate the dough into 10 individual biscuits. Flatten each biscuit out, then line the bottom and sides of 10 muffin cups. Evenly distribute sausage mixture between the cups. Mix together the eggs and milk, and divide between the cups. Sprinkle tops with shredded cheese.
4. Bake in preheated oven for 18 to 20 minutes, or until filling is set.

EASY BANANA BREAD

Servings: 24 | Prep: 20m | Cooks: 1h10m | Total: 1h30m

NUTRITION FACTS

Calories: 258 | Carbohydrates: 40.5g | Fat: 9.6g | Protein: 3.2g | Cholesterol: 31mg

INGREDIENTS

- 5 very ripe bananas
- 1 tablespoon vanilla extract
- 4 eggs
- 3 1/2 cups all-purpose flour
- 1 cup shortening

- 2 teaspoons baking soda
- 2 1/2 cups white sugar
- 1 teaspoon salt

DIRECTIONS

1. Preheat oven to 300 degrees F (150 degrees C). Grease 2 - 9x5 inch loaf pans. In a medium bowl, mash bananas and stir in the eggs until well blended. Set aside.
2. In large bowl, beat shortening and gradually add sugar. Stir in vanilla and banana mixture. Whisk together flour, baking soda, and salt; blend into batter. Add walnuts if desired. Divide between the prepared pans.
3. Bake for 1 hour 15 minutes in the preheated oven, or until a toothpick inserted into the center of the loaf comes out clean.

FRENCH CREPES

Servings: 12 | Prep: 5m | Cooks: 30m | Total: 35m

NUTRITION FACTS

Calories: 94 | Carbohydrates: 10.3g | Fat: 4.1g | Protein: 4g | Cholesterol: 55mg

INGREDIENTS

- 1 cup all-purpose flour
- 3 eggs
- 1 teaspoon white sugar
- 2 cups milk
- 1/4 teaspoon salt
- 2 tablespoons butter, melted

DIRECTIONS

1. Sift together flour, sugar and salt; set aside. In a large bowl, beat eggs and milk together with an electric mixer. Beat in flour mixture until smooth; stir in melted butter.
2. Heat a lightly oiled griddle or frying pan over medium high heat. Pour or scoop the batter onto the griddle, using approximately 2 tablespoons for each crepe. Tip and rotate pan to spread batter as thinly as possible. Brown on both sides and serve hot.

DUTCH BABIES

Servings: 2 | Prep: 8m | Cooks: 12m | Total: 20m

NUTRITION FACTS

Calories: 349 | Carbohydrates: 34.7g | Fat: 18.2g | Protein: 11.7g | Cholesterol: 221mg

INGREDIENTS

- 2 eggs
- 1 pinch salt
- 1/2 cup milk
- 2 tablespoons butter
- 1/2 cup sifted all-purpose flour
- 2 tablespoons confectioners' sugar for dusting
- 1 pinch ground nutmeg

DIRECTIONS

1. Place a 10 inch cast iron skillet inside oven and preheat oven to 475 degrees F (245 degrees C).
2. In a medium bowl, beat eggs with a whisk until light. Add milk and stir. Gradually whisk in flour, nutmeg and salt.
3. Remove skillet from oven and reduce oven heat to 425 degrees F (220 degrees C). Melt butter in hot skillet so that inside of skillet is completely coated with butter. Pour all the batter in the skillet and return skillet to oven.
4. Bake until puffed and lightly browned, about 12 minutes. Remove promptly and sprinkle with powdered sugar.

OVEN SCRAMBLED EGGS

Servings: 12 | Prep: 10m | Cooks: 25m | Total: 35m

NUTRITION FACTS

Calories: 236 | Carbohydrates: 3.2g | Fat: 18.6g | Protein: 14.3g | Cholesterol: 396mg

INGREDIENTS

- 1/2 cup butter or margarine, melted
- 2 1/4 teaspoons salt
- 24 eggs
- 2 1/2 cups milk

DIRECTIONS

1. Preheat the oven to 350 degrees F (175 degrees C).
2. Pour melted butter into a glass 9x13 inch baking dish. In a large bowl, whisk together eggs and salt until well blended. Gradually whisk in milk. Pour egg mixture into the baking dish.
3. Bake uncovered for 10 minutes, then stir, and bake an additional 10 to 15 minutes, or until eggs are set. Serve immediately.

CHARLESTON BREAKFAST CASSEROLE

Servings: 8 | Prep: 20m | Cooks: 50m | Total: 1h20m | Additional: 10m

NUTRITION FACTS

Calories: 388 | Carbohydrates: 10.8g | Fat: 1.3g | Protein: 19.4g | Cholesterol: 168mg

INGREDIENTS

- 12 slices bacon
- 1 3/4 cups milk
- 1/4 cup butter, melted
- 1 bell pepper (any color), diced
- 3 cups croutons
- 1 tablespoon prepared mustard
- 2 cups grated Cheddar cheese
- salt and pepper to taste
- 6 eggs

DIRECTIONS

1. Place bacon in a large, deep skillet. Cook over medium high heat until evenly brown. Drain, crumble and set aside.
2. Preheat oven to 325 degrees F (165 degrees C).
3. Melt butter in the microwave, or in a small pan on the stove over low heat. Spray a 9x12 inch baking dish with vegetable spray. Place croutons in the bottom of the dish, and drizzle with melted butter. Sprinkle with grated Cheddar cheese.
4. Crack the eggs into a bowl, whisking to break up the yolks. Add milk, peppers, mustard, salt, and pepper, and beat until well-combined. Pour over the croutons and cheese, and sprinkle with crumbled bacon.
5. Bake in the preheated oven for 40 minutes. Remove from oven and allow to stand 10 minutes before serving.

EASY BACON AND CHEESE QUICHE

Servings: 6 | Prep: 10m | Cooks: 50m | Total: 1h

NUTRITION FACTS

Calories: 462 | Carbohydrates: 20.2g | Fat: 31.5g | Protein: 24.7g | Cholesterol: 183mg

INGREDIENTS

- 1 (9 inch) deep dish frozen pie crust
- 3 ounces grated Parmesan cheese
- 1 (3 ounce) can bacon bits
- 4 eggs, lightly beaten
- 1/2 cup chopped onion
- 1 cup half-and-half cream
- 5 ounces shredded Swiss cheese

DIRECTIONS

1. Preheat oven to 400 degrees F (200 degrees C).
2. Place unthawed pie crust on a baking sheet. In a medium bowl, mix the bacon, onions, and both cheeses. Pour this mixture into the crust.
3. Mix the eggs and half and half in a bowl. Pour the egg mixture over the cheese mixture.
4. Bake in preheated oven for 15 minutes. Reduce heat to 350 degrees F (175 degrees C) and bake for an additional 35 minutes, until top of quiche begins to turn brown.

DELICIOUS PUMPKIN BREAD

Servings: 24 | Prep: 10m | Cooks: 1h | Total: 1h10m

NUTRITION FACTS

Calories: 275 | Carbohydrates: 40.1g | Fat: 11.9g | Protein: 3..4g | Cholesterol: 31mg

INGREDIENTS

- 3 1/4 cups all-purpose flour
- 2 cups solid pack pumpkin puree
- 3 cups white sugar
- 2/3 cup water
- 2 teaspoons baking soda
- 1 cup vegetable oil
- 1 1/2 teaspoons salt
- 4 eggs
- 1 teaspoon ground nutmeg
- 1/2 cup chopped walnuts (optional)
- 1 teaspoon ground cinnamon

DIRECTIONS

1. Grease and flour three 7 x 3 inch pans. Preheat oven to 350 degrees F (175 degrees C).

2. Measure flour, sugar, baking soda, salt, and spices into a large bowl. Stir to blend. Add pumpkin, water, vegetable oil, eggs, and nuts. Beat until well combined. Pour batter into prepared pans.
3. Bake for approximately 1 hour.

SCRAMBLED EGGS DONE RIGHT
Servings: 1 | Prep: 2m | Cooks: 4m | Total: 6m

NUTRITION FACTS

Calories: 210 | Carbohydrates: 1g | Fat: 17.4g | Protein: 12.7g | Cholesterol: 374mg

INGREDIENTS

- 2 eggs
- 1 teaspoon margarine or butter
- 1 teaspoon mayonnaise or salad dressing
- salt and pepper to taste (optional)
- 1 teaspoon water (optional)

DIRECTIONS

1. In a cup or small bowl, whisk together the eggs, mayonnaise and water using a fork. Melt margarine in a skillet over low heat. Pour in the eggs, and stir constantly as they cook. Remove the eggs to a plate when they are set, but still moist. Do not over cook. Never add salt or pepper until eggs are on plate, but these are also good without.

SPINACH AND POTATO FRITTATA
Servings: 6 | Prep: 10m | Cooks: 20m | Total: 30m

NUTRITION FACTS

Calories: 281 | Carbohydrates: 28.7g | Fat: 13.1g | Protein: 12.5g | Cholesterol: 197mg

INGREDIENTS

- 2 tablespoons olive oil
- salt and pepper to taste
- 6 small red potatoes, sliced
- 6 eggs
- 1 cup torn fresh spinach
- 1/3 cup milk
- 2 tablespoons sliced green onions

- 1/2 cup shredded Cheddar cheese
- 1 teaspoon crushed garlic

DIRECTIONS

1. Heat olive oil in a medium skillet over medium heat. Place potatoes in the skillet, cover, and cook about 10 minutes, until tender but firm. Mix in spinach, green onions, and garlic. Season with salt and pepper. Continue cooking 1 to 2 minutes, until spinach is wilted.
2. In a medium bowl, beat together eggs and milk. Pour into the skillet over the vegetables. Sprinkle with Cheddar cheese. Reduce heat to low, cover, and cook 5 to 7 minutes, or until eggs are firm.

BUTTERMILK PANCAKES

Servings: 4 | Prep: 15m | Cooks: 15m | Total: 30m

NUTRITION FACTS

Calories: 360 | Carbohydrates: 46.3g | Fat: 15.9g | Protein: 8.1g | Cholesterol: 50mg

INGREDIENTS

- 1 1/4 cups all-purpose flour
- 1 teaspoon baking powder
- 1 egg
- 1 teaspoon baking soda
- 1 1/4 cups buttermilk
- 1/4 cup vegetable oil
- 1/4 cup white sugar

DIRECTIONS

1. Preheat a skillet over medium heat. Combine all ingredients in a blender. Puree until smooth.
2. Pour batter onto the griddle, to form 5 pancakes. Flip pancakes when edges appear to harden. Cook pancakes on other side for same amount of time until golden brown.

BUTTERSCOTCH OATMEAL

Servings: 3 | Prep: 5m | Cooks: 10m | Total: 15m

NUTRITION FACTS

Calories: 357 | Carbohydrates: 48.8g | Fat: 13.9g | Protein: 10.5g | Cholesterol: 94mg

INGREDIENTS

- 1 egg, beaten
- 1 cup rolled oats
- 1 3/4 cups milk
- 2 tablespoons butter
- 1/2 cup packed brown sugar

DIRECTIONS

1. In a saucepan over medium heat, whisk together the egg, milk and brown sugar. Mix in the oats. When the oatmeal begins to boil, cook and stir until thick. Remove from the heat, and stir in butter until melted. Serve immediately.

BAKED DENVER OMELET

Servings: 4 | Prep: 10m | Cooks: 35m | Total: 45m

NUTRITION FACTS

Calories: 345 | Carbohydrates: 3.6g | Fat: 26.8g | Protein: 22.4g | Cholesterol: 381mg

INGREDIENTS

- 2 tablespoons butter
- 8 eggs
- 1/2 onion, chopped
- 1/4 cup milk
- 1/2 green bell pepper, chopped
- 1/2 cup shredded Cheddar cheese
- 1 cup chopped cooked ham
- salt and ground black pepper to taste

DIRECTIONS

1. Preheat oven to 400 degrees F (200 degrees C). Grease a 10-inch round baking dish.
2. Melt butter in a large skillet over medium heat; cook and stir onion and bell pepper until softened, about 5 minutes. Stir in ham and continue cooking until heated through, 5 minutes more.
3. Beat eggs and milk in a large bowl. Stir in Cheddar cheese and ham mixture; season with salt and black pepper. Pour mixture into prepared baking dish.
4. Bake in preheated oven until eggs are browned and puffy, about 25 minutes. Serve warm.

EASTER BREAKFAST CASSEROLE

Servings: 12 | Prep: 12m | Cooks: 1h15m | Total: 1h40m

NUTRITION FACTS

Calories: 281 | Carbohydrates: 9.9g | Fat: 21g | Protein: 18g | Cholesterol: 171mg

INGREDIENTS

- 1 pound bacon
- 8 eggs
- 1/4 cup diced onion
- 2 cups milk
- 1/4 cup diced green bell pepper
- 1 (16 ounce) package frozen hash brown potatoes, thawed
- 3 cups shredded Cheddar cheese

DIRECTIONS

1. Preheat oven to 350 degrees F (175 degrees C). Lightly grease a 7x11 inch casserole dish.
2. Fry the bacon in a large, deep skillet over medium-high heat until evenly browned, about 10 minutes. Drain on a paper towel-lined plate. Crumble.
3. In a large bowl beat together eggs and milk. Mix in cheese, bacon, onion and green pepper. Stir in the thawed hash browns. Pour mixture into prepared casserole.
4. Cover with aluminum foil and bake in preheated oven for 45 minutes. Uncover and bake for another 30 minutes until eggs have set.

PUMPKIN PIE BREAD

Servings: 24 | Prep: 15m | Cooks: 1h | Total: 1h15m

NUTRITION FACTS

Calories: 263 | Carbohydrates: 40.6g | Fat: 10.3g | Protein: 3.1g | Cholesterol: 31mg

INGREDIENTS

- 3 1/2 cups all-purpose flour
- 3 cups white sugar
- 2 teaspoons baking soda
- 1 cup vegetable oil
- 1 teaspoon baking powder
- 4 eggs
- 3 teaspoons pumpkin pie spice
- 1 (15 ounce) can pumpkin puree
- 1 teaspoon salt
- 1/2 cup water

DIRECTIONS

1. Preheat oven to 350 degrees F (175 degrees C). Grease two 9x5 inch loaf pans. Sift together the flour, baking soda, baking powder, salt, and pumpkin pie spice. Set aside.
2. In a large bowl, beat together sugar, oil, eggs, and pumpkin. Stir in flour mixture alternately with water. Divide batter evenly between the prepared pans.
3. Bake in the preheated oven for 60 to 70 minutes, or until a toothpick inserted into the center comes out clean. For best flavor, store wrapped in plastic wrap at room temperature for a full day before serving.

CRAB QUICHE
Servings: 8 | Prep: 10m | Cooks: 45m | Total: 1h

NUTRITION FACTS

Calories: 326 | Carbohydrates: 14.3g | Fat: 24.8g | Protein: 11.8g | Cholesterol: 83mg

INGREDIENTS

- 1/2 cup mayonnaise
- 1 cup crab meat
- 2 tablespoons all-purpose flour
- 1 cup diced Swiss cheese
- 2 eggs, beaten
- 1/2 cup chopped green onions
- 1/2 cup milk
- 1 (9 inch) unbaked pie crust

DIRECTIONS

1. Preheat oven to 350 degrees F (175 degrees C).
2. In a medium bowl, beat together eggs, mayonnaise, flour, and milk until thoroughly blended. Stir in crab, cheese, and onion. Spread into pie shell.
3. Bake for 40 to 45 minutes, or until a knife inserted in the center comes out clean.

SPINACH QUICHE WITH COTTAGE CHEESE
Servings: 4 | Prep: 15m | Cooks: 10m | Total: 45m

NUTRITION FACTS

Calories: 231 | Carbohydrates: 6.1g | Fat: 14.9g | Protein: 19.1g | Cholesterol: 131mg

INGREDIENTS

- 1 (10 ounce) package frozen chopped spinach, thawed
- 1 (16 ounce) package cottage cheese
- 1 bunch green onions, finely chopped (white parts only)
- 2 cups shredded Cheddar cheese
- 4 eggs, beaten
- 1/4 cup crushed croutons

DIRECTIONS

1. Preheat oven to 325 degrees F (165 degrees C). Lightly grease a 9 inch pie or quiche pan.
2. Place spinach in a small saucepan. Cook over medium heat, stirring occasionally until soft. Drain off any remaining liquid. Stir in green onions, eggs, cottage cheese and Cheddar cheese. Pour mixture into prepared pan.
3. Bake uncovered in preheated oven for 45 minutes. Remove from oven and sprinkle with crushed croutons. Return to oven and bake for an additional 15 minutes, until eggs are set.

FRENCH TOAST

Servings: 4 | Prep: 10m | Cooks: 25m | Total: 35m

NUTRITION FACTS

Calories: 341 | Carbohydrates: 52.2g | Fat: 8.6g | Protein: 13.7g | Cholesterol: 190mg

INGREDIENTS

- 4 eggs
- 1 teaspoon ground nutmeg
- 3/4 cup milk
- 12 slices white bread
- 3 tablespoons brown sugar
- 1 tablespoon ground cinnamon

DIRECTIONS

1. In a large mixing bowl, beat the eggs. Add the milk, brown sugar and nutmeg; stir well to combine.
2. Soak bread slices in the egg mixture until saturated.
3. Heat a lightly oiled griddle or frying pan over medium high heat. Brown slices on both sides, sprinkle with cinnamon and serve hot.

EGGS BENEDICT

Servings: 4 | Prep: 25m | Cooks: 5m | Total: 30m

NUTRITION FACTS

Calories: 879 | Carbohydrates: 29.6g | Fat: 71.1g | Protein: 31.8g | Cholesterol: 742mg

INGREDIENTS

- 4 egg yolks
- 1/4 teaspoon salt
- 3 1/2 tablespoons lemon juice
- 8 eggs
- 1 pinch ground white pepper
- 1 teaspoon distilled white vinegar
- 1/8 teaspoon Worcestershire sauce
- 8 strips Canadian-style bacon
- 1 tablespoon water
- 4 English muffins, split
- 1 cup butter, melted
- 2 tablespoons butter, softened

DIRECTIONS

1. To Make Hollandaise: Fill the bottom of a double boiler part-way with water. Make sure that water does not touch the top pan. Bring water to a gentle simmer. In the top of the double boiler, whisk together egg yolks, lemon juice, white pepper, Worcestershire sauce, and 1 tablespoon water.
2. Add the melted butter to egg yolk mixture 1 or 2 tablespoons at a time while whisking yolks constantly. If hollandaise begins to get too thick, add a teaspoon or two of hot water. Continue whisking until all butter is incorporated. Whisk in salt, then remove from heat. Place a lid on pan to keep sauce warm.
3. Preheat oven on broiler setting. To Poach Eggs: Fill a large saucepan with 3 inches of water. Bring water to a gentle simmer, then add vinegar. Carefully break eggs into simmering water, and allow to cook for 2 1/2 to 3 minutes. Yolks should still be soft in center. Remove eggs from water with a slotted spoon and set on a warm plate.
4. While eggs are poaching, brown the bacon in a medium skillet over medium-high heat and toast the English muffins on a baking sheet under the broiler.
5. Spread toasted muffins with softened butter, and top each one with a slice of bacon, followed by one poached egg. Place 2 muffins on each plate and drizzle with hollandaise sauce. Sprinkle with chopped chives and serve immediately.

LOLA'S HORCHATA

Servings: 6 | Prep: 10m | Cooks: 3h | Total: 3h10m

NUTRITION FACTS

Calories: 213 | Carbohydrates: 48.4g | Fat: 0.6g | Protein: 2.9g | Cholesterol: 2mg

INGREDIENTS

- 1 cup uncooked white long-grain rice
- 1/2 tablespoon vanilla extract
- 5 cups water
- 1/2 tablespoon ground cinnamon
- 1/2 cup milk
- 2/3 cup white sugar

DIRECTIONS

1. Pour the rice and water into the bowl of a blender; blend until the rice just begins to break up, about 1 minute. Let rice and water stand at room temperature for a minimum of 3 hours.
2. Strain the rice water into a pitcher and discard the rice. Stir the milk, vanilla, cinnamon, and sugar into the rice water. Chill and stir before serving over ice.

QUICK AND EASY HOME FRIES

Servings: 4 | Prep: 5m | Cooks: 20m | Total: 25m

NUTRITION FACTS

Calories: 199 | Carbohydrates: 27.9g | Fat: 8.8g | Protein: 3.3g | Cholesterol: 23mg

INGREDIENTS

- 3 medium russet potatoes, cubed
- salt and pepper to taste
- 3 tablespoons butter or margarine

DIRECTIONS

1. Rinse potato cubes with cold water, and drain well. Melt butter or margarine in a large skillet over medium heat. Place potatoes in the skillet, and stir to coat with butter. Season with salt and pepper. Cover with a lid, and cook for 10 minutes. Remove the lid, and cook for another 10 minutes, turning frequently until brown and crisp on all sides.

BREAKFAST CASSEROLE

Servings: 12 | Prep: 15m | Cooks: 1h | Total: 1h15m

NUTRITION FACTS

Calories: 352 | Carbohydrates: 22.8g | Fat: 23.8g | Protein: 15.8g | Cholesterol: 215mg

INGREDIENTS

- 1 (16 ounce) package ground pork breakfast sausage
- 1 (4.5 ounce) can sliced mushrooms, drained
- 12 eggs
- 1 (32 ounce) package frozen potato rounds
- 1 (10.75 ounce) can condensed cream of mushroom soup
- 1/2 cup shredded Cheddar cheese
- 1 1/4 cups milk

DIRECTIONS

1. Place sausage in a skillet over medium-high heat, and cook until evenly brown. Drain, and set aside.
2. Preheat oven to 350 degrees F (175 degrees C). Lightly grease a 9x13 inch baking dish.
3. In a large bowl, beat together the eggs, condensed cream of mushroom soup, and milk. Stir in the sausage and mushrooms, and pour into the prepared baking dish. Mix in the frozen potato rounds.
4. Bake in preheated oven for 45 to 50 minutes. Sprinkle with cheese, and bake an additional 10 minutes, or until cheese is melted.

WHEAT GERM WHOLE-WHEAT BUTTERMILK PANCAKES

Servings: 12 | Prep: 10m | Cooks: 10m | Total: 20m

NUTRITION FACTS

Calories: 128 | Carbohydrates: 13.2g | Fat: 6.5g | Protein: 5g | Cholesterol: 33mg

INGREDIENTS

- 2 eggs, lightly beaten
- 1/2 cup wheat germ
- 1/4 cup canola oil
- 1/2 teaspoon salt
- 2 cups buttermilk
- 1 1/2 cups whole wheat pastry flour
- 2 teaspoons baking soda

DIRECTIONS

1. In a medium bowl, mix eggs with oil and buttermilk. Stir in baking soda, wheat germ, salt and flour; mix until blended.

2. Heat a lightly oiled griddle or frying pan over medium-high heat. Pour or scoop the batter onto the griddle, using approximately 1/4 cup for each pancake. Brown on both sides, turning once.

APPLE BREAKFAST BREAD

Servings: 10 | Prep: 15m | Cooks: 1h | Total: 1h30m | Additional: 15m

NUTRITION FACTS

Calories: 279 | Carbohydrates: 43.2g | Fat: 10.5g | Protein: 4g | Cholesterol: 62mg

INGREDIENTS

- 1/2 cup butter
- 1/2 teaspoon salt
- 1 cup sugar
- 1 teaspoon ground cinnamon
- 2 eggs
- 1/2 teaspoon ground cloves
- 2 cups all-purpose flour
- 2 apples - peeled, cored and chopped
- 1 teaspoon baking soda

DIRECTIONS

1. Preheat oven to 350 degrees F (175 degrees C). Lightly grease an 8x4 inch loaf pan.
2. In a bowl, mix the butter and sugar until smooth and creamy. Beat in the eggs.
3. In a separate bowl, sift together the flour, baking soda, salt, cinnamon, and cloves. Mix into the butter mixture until moistened. Fold in the apples. Transfer to the prepared loaf pan.
4. Bake 1 hour in the preheated oven, until a toothpick inserted in the center comes out clean. Cool in the pan for 15 minutes before removing to a wire rack to cool completely.

MAKE AHEAD FRENCH TOAST

Servings: 8 | Prep: 15m | Cooks: 45m | Total: 14h10m

NUTRITION FACTS

Calories: 503 | Carbohydrates: 51.8g | Fat: 29.3g | Protein: 11g | Cholesterol: 162mg

INGREDIENTS

- 5 eggs, lightly beaten
- 1/2 cup butter, melted
- 1 1/2 cups milk

- 1 cup light brown sugar
- 1 cup half-and-half cream
- 2 tablespoons maple syrup
- 1 teaspoon vanilla extract
- 1 cup chopped pecans
- 1/2 (1 pound) loaf French bread, cut diagonally in 1 inch slices

DIRECTIONS

1. In a large bowl, whisk together eggs, milk, cream and vanilla. Dip bread slices into egg mixture and place in a lightly greased 9x13 inch baking pan. Refrigerate overnight.
2. The next morning: Preheat oven to 350 degrees F (175 degrees C).
3. In a small bowl, combine butter, sugar, maple syrup and pecans. Spoon mixture over bread.
4. Bake in preheated oven until golden, about 40 minutes. Let stand 5 minutes before serving.

ASPARAGUS QUICHE

Servings: 12 | Prep: 25m | Cooks: 35m | Total: 1h

NUTRITION FACTS

Calories: 334 | Carbohydrates: 12.4g | Fat: 26.3g | Protein: 12.4g | Cholesterol: 106mg

INGREDIENTS

- 1 pound fresh asparagus, trimmed and cut into 1/2 inch pieces
- 1 1/2 cups half-and-half cream
- 10 slices bacon
- 1/4 teaspoon ground nutmeg
- 2 (8 inch) unbaked pie shells
- salt and pepper to taste
- 1 egg white, lightly beaten
- 2 cups shredded Swiss cheese
- 4 eggs

DIRECTIONS

1. Preheat oven to 400 degrees F (200 degrees C). Place asparagus in a steamer over 1 inch of boiling water, and cover. Cook until tender but still firm, about 2 to 6 minutes. Drain and cool.
2. Place bacon in a large, deep skillet. Cook over medium high heat until evenly brown. Drain, crumble and set aside.
3. Brush pie shells with beaten egg white. Sprinkle crumbled bacon and chopped asparagus into pie shells.

4. In a bowl, beat together eggs, cream, nutmeg, salt and pepper. Sprinkle Swiss cheese over bacon and asparagus. Pour egg mixture on top of cheese.
5. Bake uncovered in preheated oven until firm, about 35 to 40 minutes. Let cool to room temperature before serving.

OATMEAL AND WHEAT FLOUR BLUEBERRY PANCAKES
Servings: 8 | Prep: 10m | Cooks: 20m | Total: 30m

NUTRITION FACTS

Calories: 250 | Carbohydrates: 30.8g | Fat: 10.9g | Protein: 8.2g | Cholesterol: 70mg

INGREDIENTS

- 1/2 cup whole wheat flour
- 1 1/2 cups quick cooking oats
- 1/2 cup all-purpose flour
- 2 cups soy milk
- 2 tablespoons brown sugar
- 3 eggs, beaten
- 2 tablespoons baking powder
- 1/4 cup olive oil
- 3/4 teaspoon salt
- 1/2 cup frozen blueberries

DIRECTIONS

1. Preheat a lightly oiled griddle over medium heat.
2. In a large bowl, mix whole wheat flour, all-purpose flour, brown sugar, baking powder, and salt.
3. In a small bowl, mix oats and soy milk. Whisk in eggs and olive oil. Pour into the flour mixture all at once. Continue mixing until smooth. Gently fold in blueberries.
4. Pour batter about 1/4 cup at a time onto the prepared griddle. Cook 1 to 2 minutes, until bubbly. Flip, and continue cooking until lightly browned.

QUICHE
Servings: 8 | Prep: 20m | Cooks: 1h | Total: 1h20m

NUTRITION FACTS

Calories: 260 | Carbohydrates: 14.1g | Fat: 17.2g | Protein: 12g | Cholesterol: 96mg

INGREDIENTS

- 1 1/2 cups shredded Swiss cheese

- 1/4 teaspoon salt
- 4 teaspoons all-purpose flour
- 1/4 teaspoon ground dry mustard
- 1/2 cup cooked ham, diced
- 1 (9 inch) unbaked pie crust
- 3 eggs
- 2 tablespoons chopped fresh parsley, for garnish
- 1 cup milk
- 2 tablespoons chopped pimento peppers, garnish

DIRECTIONS

1. In medium bowl, toss 4 teaspoons flour with the grated cheese. Sprinkle mixture into the pie shell. On top of cheese, sprinkle 1/2 cup of diced ham.
2. In medium bowl, combine eggs, milk or cream, and then add salt and mustard powder. Beat until smooth and pour over cheese and ham.
3. Put piece of plastic wrap large enough to overlap sides over top of quiche, then a piece of foil, and seal well around the edges. (plastic keeps the foil from sticking to the food). Place prepared quiche in freezer.
4. When ready to prepare, preheat oven to 400 degrees F (200 degrees C.) Remove foil and plastic wrap. Put foil around edge of crust to protect it.
5. Bake in the preheated oven for 60 minutes, or until filling is set and crust is golden brown. Garnish with parsley and pimiento if desired.

WAFFLES

Servings: 4 | Prep: 5m | Cooks: 15m | Total: 20m

NUTRITION FACTS

Calories: 491 | Carbohydrates: 53.1g | Fat: 25.3g | Protein: 12.6g | Cholesterol: 100mg

INGREDIENTS

- 2 cups all-purpose flour
- 1 1/2 cups milk
- 4 teaspoons baking powder
- 6 tablespoons vegetable oil
- 1/4 teaspoon salt
- 2 eggs, separated

DIRECTIONS

1. Preheat waffle iron. In a large mixing bowl, sift together flour, baking powder and salt. Stir in milk, oil and egg yolks until mixture is smooth. In a separate bowl, beat egg whites until soft peaks form. Gently fold egg whites into batter.
2. Spray preheated waffle iron with non-stick cooking spray. Pour mix onto hot waffle iron. Cook until golden; serve hot.

MOM'S BEST WAFFLES

Servings: 4 | Prep: 5m | Cooks: 10m | Total: 15m

NUTRITION FACTS

Calories: 410 | Carbohydrates: 60.3g | Fat: 12.3g | Protein: 13.6g | Cholesterol: 103mg

INGREDIENTS

- 2 cups all-purpose flour
- 2 cups milk
- 2 teaspoons baking powder
- 2 eggs
- 2 tablespoons white sugar
- 2 tablespoons vegetable oil
- 1 teaspoon salt

DIRECTIONS

1. In a large bowl, stir together flour, baking powder, sugar and salt. Add milk, eggs and oil; mix well.
2. Spray preheated waffle iron with non-stick cooking spray. Pour mix onto hot waffle iron. Cook until golden brown.

CHRISTMAS BRUNCH CASSEROLE

Servings: 5 | Prep: 40m | Cooks: 1h | Total: 1d | Additional: 1d

NUTRITION FACTS

Calories: 494 | Carbohydrates: 31.9g | Fat: 28.6 g | Protein: 28.1g | Cholesterol: 217mg

INGREDIENTS

- 1 pound bacon
- 1/4 teaspoon garlic salt
- 2 onions, chopped
- 1/2 teaspoon ground black pepper
- 2 cups fresh sliced mushrooms
- 4 eggs

- 1 tablespoon butter
- 1 1/2 cups milk
- 4 cups frozen hash brown potatoes, thawed
- 1 pinch dried parsley
- 1 teaspoon salt
- 1 cup shredded Cheddar cheese

DIRECTIONS

1. Place bacon in a large skillet. Cook over medium-high heat until evenly brown. Drain and set aside. Add the mushrooms and onion to the skillet; cook and stir until the onion has softened and turned translucent and the mushrooms are tender, about 5 minutes.
2. Grease a 9x13-inch casserole dish with the tablespoon of butter. Place potatoes in bottom of prepared dish. Sprinkle with salt, garlic salt, and pepper. Top with crumbled bacon, then add the onions and mushrooms.
3. In a mixing bowl, beat the eggs with the milk and parsley. Pour the beaten eggs over the casserole and top with grated cheese. Cover and refrigerate overnight.
4. Preheat oven to 400 degrees F (200 degrees C).
5. Bake in preheated oven for 1 hour or until set.

CHUNKY MONKEY PANCAKES
Servings: 9 | Prep: 10m | Cooks: 20m | Total: 30m

NUTRITION FACTS

Calories: 195 | Carbohydrates: 23.4g | Fat: 10.2g | Protein: 4.4g | Cholesterol: 52mg

INGREDIENTS

- 1 cup all-purpose flour
- 1 tablespoon white sugar
- 2 teaspoons baking powder
- 1 teaspoon vanilla extract
- 1 teaspoon baking soda
- 1 large banana, diced
- 1/4 teaspoon salt
- 1/2 cup miniature semisweet chocolate chips
- 3/4 cup skim milk
- 1/4 cup chopped pecans
- 3 tablespoons butter, melted
- cooking spray

- 2 eggs

DIRECTIONS

1. Combine flour, baking powder, baking soda, and salt in a large bowl. Set bowl aside. In a separate bowl, whisk together the skim milk, melted butter, eggs, sugar, and vanilla. Make a well in the center of the dry ingredients and stir in the wet ingredients, being careful not to over mix the batter. Gently fold in the banana, chocolate chips, and nuts.
2. Heat a large skillet over medium heat, and coat with cooking spray. Pour 1/4 cupfuls of batter onto the skillet, and cook until bubbles appear on the surface. Flip with a spatula, and cook until browned on the other side.

GERMAN PANCAKES

Servings: 6 | Prep: 15m | Cooks: 40m | Total: 55m

NUTRITION FACTS

Calories: 235 | Carbohydrates: 18.2g | Fat: 13.6g | Protein: 9.9g | Cholesterol: 210mg

INGREDIENTS

- 1/4 cup butter
- 6 eggs, lightly beaten
- 1 cup all-purpose flour
- 1/8 teaspoon salt
- 1 cup milk

DIRECTIONS

1. Preheat oven to 350 degrees F (175 degrees C). Melt butter in a medium baking dish.
2. In a medium bowl, mix flour, milk, eggs and salt. Pour the mixture into the prepared baking dish.
3. Bake on center rack in the preheated oven for 30 to 40 minutes, until golden brown.

BROWN SUGAR BANANA NUT BREAD

Servings: 12 | Prep: 15m | Cooks: 1h | Total: 1h15m

NUTRITION FACTS

Calories: 273 | Carbohydrates: 37.9g | Fat: 12.1g | Protein: 4.5g | Cholesterol: 51mg

INGREDIENTS

- 1/2 cup butter, softened
- 2 cups all-purpose flour
- 1 cup brown sugar

- 3 teaspoons baking powder
- 2 eggs
- 1/2 teaspoon salt
- 1 tablespoon vanilla extract
- 1/2 cup chopped walnuts
- 4 very ripe bananas, mashed

DIRECTIONS

1. Preheat oven to 350 degrees F (175 degrees C). Lightly grease a 9x5 inch loaf pan.
2. In a large bowl, cream together the butter and sugar until light and fluffy. Stir in the eggs one at a time, beating well with each addition. Stir in vanilla and banana. In a separate bowl, sift together flour, baking powder, and salt.
3. Blend the banana mixture into the flour mixture; stir just to combine. Fold in walnuts. Pour batter into prepared pan.
4. Bake in preheated oven for 1 hour, until a toothpick inserted into center of loaf comes out clean.

LOWER FAT BANANA BREAD

Servings: 12 | Prep: 15m | Cooks: 1h | Total: 1h15m

NUTRITION FACTS

Calories: 169 | Carbohydrates: 28.8g | Fat: 4.9g | Protein: 3.1g | Cholesterol: 31mg

INGREDIENTS

- 2/3 cup white sugar
- 1 2/3 cups all-purpose flour
- 1/4 cup margarine, softened
- 1 teaspoon baking soda
- 2 eggs
- 1/2 teaspoon salt
- 1 cup mashed bananas
- 1/4 teaspoon baking powder
- 1/4 cup water

DIRECTIONS

1. Preheat oven to 350 degrees F (175 degrees C). Spray one 9x5x3 inch loaf pan with a non-stick cooking spray.
2. In a medium bowl, beat the white sugar and margarine or butter until smooth and creamy. Beat in the eggs, water and bananas with the sugar mixture until it is well blended.

3. Mix in the flour, baking soda, salt and baking powder just until the mixture is moistened. Be sure to scrape the sides of the bowl to blend all ingredients.
4. Bake at 350 degrees F (175 degree C) for about 60 minutes. Bread is done when the top is firm to the touch and a golden brown color. Time will vary according to loaf size and oven type. When bread is removed from oven, allow it to cool on it's side for 10 minutes, then remove from pan and let cool on a rack. This bread is also excellent if you add mini chocolate chips or small fruit pieces to the mix just before baking.

BAKED OMELET

Servings: 4 | Prep: 15m | Cooks: 40m | Total: 55m

NUTRITION FACTS

Calories: 314 | Carbohydrates: 5.9g | Fat: 21.2g | Protein: 24.8g | Cholesterol: 415mg

INGREDIENTS

- 8 eggs
- 1/2 cup shredded Cheddar cheese
- 1 cup milk
- 1/2 cup shredded mozzarella cheese
- 1/2 teaspoon seasoning salt
- 1 tablespoon dried minced onion
- 3 ounces cooked ham, diced

DIRECTIONS

1. Preheat oven to 350 degrees F (175 degrees C). Grease one 8x8 inch casserole dish and set aside.
2. Beat together the eggs and milk. Add seasoning salt, ham, Cheddar cheese, Mozzarella cheese and minced onion. Pour into prepared casserole dish.
3. Bake uncovered at 350 degrees F (175 degrees C) for 40 to 45 minutes.

EASY SPICY ROASTED POTATOES

Servings: 4 | Prep: 15m | Cooks: 40m | Total: 55m

NUTRITION FACTS

Calories: 473 | Carbohydrates: 47.6g | Fat: 26.1g | Protein: 14.4g | Cholesterol: 36mg

INGREDIENTS

- 5 medium red potatoes, diced with peel

- 2 teaspoons chili powder
- 1 medium onion, chopped
- 1/4 cup extra virgin olive oil
- 1 tablespoon garlic powder
- 1 cup shredded Cheddar cheese (optional)
- 1 tablespoon kosher salt

DIRECTIONS

1. Preheat the oven to 450 degrees F (220 degrees C).
2. Arrange the potatoes and onions in a greased 9x13 inch baking dish so that they are evenly distributed. Season with garlic powder, salt and chili powder. Drizzle with olive oil. Stir to coat potatoes and onions with oil and spices.
3. Bake for 35 to 40 minutes in the preheated oven, until potatoes are fork tender and slightly crispy. Stir every 10 minutes. When done, sprinkle with cheese. Wait about 5 minutes for the cheese to melt before serving.

APPLE RAISIN FRENCH TOAST STRATA

Servings: 12 | Prep: 20m | Cooks: 45m | Total: 3h15m

NUTRITION FACTS

Calories: 354 | Carbohydrates: 28.3g | Fat: 23.1g | Protein: 10.1g | Cholesterol: 178mg

INGREDIENTS

- 1 (1 pound) loaf cinnamon raisin bread, cubed
- 2 1/2 cups half-and-half cream
- 1 (8 ounce) package cream cheese, diced
- 6 tablespoons butter, melted
- 1 cup diced peeled apples
- 1/4 cup maple syrup
- 8 eggs

DIRECTIONS

1. Coat a 9x13 inch baking dish with cooking spray. Arrange 1/2 of the cubed raisin bread in the bottom of the dish. Sprinkle the cream cheese evenly over the bread, and top with the apples. If you like extra raisins, add them now. Top with remaining bread.
2. In a large bowl, beat the eggs with the cream, butter, and maple syrup. Pour over the bread mixture. Cover with plastic wrap, and press down so that all bread pieces are soaked. Refrigerate at least 2 hours.
3. Preheat oven to 325 degrees F (165 degrees C).

4. Bake 45 minutes in the preheated oven. Let stand for 10 minutes before serving.

EGG IN A HOLE

Servings: 1 | Prep: 1m | Cooks: 4m | Total: 5m

NUTRITION FACTS

Calories: 231 | Carbohydrates: 13.1g | Fat: 15.9g | Protein: 8.7g | Cholesterol: 208mg

INGREDIENTS

- 1 1/2 teaspoons bacon grease
- 1 egg
- 1 slice bread
- salt and ground black pepper to taste

DIRECTIONS

1. Melt the bacon grease in a non-stick pan over low heat.
2. Cut a 1 1/2 to 2-inch hole from the center of the bread slice; lay in the hot skillet. When the side facing down is lightly toasted, about 2 minutes, flip and crack the egg into the hole; season with salt and pepper. Continue to cook until the egg is cooked and mostly firm. Flip again and cook 1 minute more to assure doneness on both sides. Serve immediately.

WHOLE WHEAT, OATMEAL, AND BANANA PANCAKES

Servings: 6 | Prep: 15m | Cooks: 15m | Total: 30m

NUTRITION FACTS

Calories: 333 | Carbohydrates: 54.7g | Fat: 8.5g | Protein: 11g | Cholesterol: 38mg

INGREDIENTS

- 1 cup uncooked rolled oats
- 1/2 teaspoon salt
- 1 cup whole wheat flour
- 1 egg
- 3/4 cup all-purpose flour
- 2 cups milk
- 1/4 cup brown sugar
- 2 tablespoons vegetable oil
- 2 tablespoons dry milk powder
- 1 teaspoon vanilla extract

- 2 teaspoons baking powder
- 1 banana, mashed
- 1/2 teaspoon baking soda

DIRECTIONS

1. Place the rolled oats into the jar of a blender and blend until the texture resembles coarse flour. Whisk together the blended oats, whole wheat flour, all-purpose flour, brown sugar, dry milk powder, baking powder, baking soda, and salt in a bowl; set aside.
2. Whisk together the egg, milk, vegetable oil, and vanilla. Stir in the mashed banana. Pour the egg mixture into the flour mixture and stir just until moistened. Let the batter stand for 5 minutes.
3. Heat a lightly oiled griddle over medium-high heat. Drop batter by large spoonfuls onto the griddle, and cook until bubbles form and the edges are dry, about 2 minutes. Flip, and cook until browned on the other side. Repeat with remaining batter.

MOM'S APPLESAUCE PANCAKES

Servings: 4 | Prep: 10m | Cooks: 20m | Total: 30m

NUTRITION FACTS

Calories: 319 | Carbohydrates: 60.2g | Fat: 4.3g | Protein: 10.1g | Cholesterol: 95mg

INGREDIENTS

- 2 cups dry pancake mix
- 1 cup applesauce
- 1 teaspoon ground cinnamon
- 1 teaspoon lemon juice
- 2 eggs
- 1/2 cup milk

DIRECTIONS

1. In a large bowl, stir together pancake mix and cinnamon. Make a well in the center of the pancake mix. Add the eggs, applesauce, lemon juice and milk; stir until smooth.
2. Heat a lightly oiled griddle or frying pan over medium high heat. Pour or scoop the batter onto the griddle, using approximately 1/4 cup for each pancake. Brown on both sides and serve hot.

BAKED OATMEAL

Servings: 8 | Prep: 10m | Cooks: 35m | Total: 45m

NUTRITION FACTS

Calories: 378 | Carbohydrates: 49.8g | Fat: 17.8g | Protein: 6.7g | Cholesterol: 49mg

INGREDIENTS

- 1/2 cup vegetable oil
- 1 tablespoon baking powder
- 3/4 cup white sugar
- 3 cups quick cooking oats
- 2 eggs
- 1/2 cup raisins
- 1 cup milk
- 2 tablespoons brown sugar
- 1/2 teaspoon salt
- 1/2 teaspoon ground cinnamon

DIRECTIONS

1. Beat together oil and sugar. Mix in eggs, milk, salt, baking powder, oatmeal. Beat well then stir in raisins. Pour into a lightly grease pie pan. Sprinkle with brown sugar and cinnamon. Refrigerate overnight.
2. The next morning, preheat oven to 350 degrees F (175 degrees C).
3. Bake in preheated oven until firm, about 35 minutes. Serve hot.

BANANA NUT BREAD

Servings: 24 | Prep: 10m | Cooks: 1h | Total: 1h10m

NUTRITION FACTS

Calories: 256 | Carbohydrates: 37.1g | Fat: 11.1g | Protein: 3.3g | Cholesterol: 24mg

INGREDIENTS

- 2 1/2 cups white sugar
- 1 1/4 cups buttermilk
- 1 cup shortening
- 1 1/2 teaspoons baking soda
- 3 eggs
- 1 1/2 teaspoons baking powder
- 1 1/2 cups mashed bananas
- 1 teaspoon vanilla extract
- 3 cups all-purpose flour
- 1/2 cup chopped walnuts

DIRECTIONS

1. Preheat oven to 350 degrees F (175 degrees C).

2. Cream together shortening and sugar. Add eggs one at a time, beating well after each addition. Mix in bananas, buttermilk, and vanilla. Mix in flour, baking powder, and soda. Stir in nuts if desired. Pour batter into two greased 9x5 inch pans.
3. Bake for 50 to 60 minutes in the preheated oven, or until a toothpick inserted into the center of the loaf comes out clean.

APPLE-RAISIN FRENCH TOAST CASSEROLE
Servings: 12 | Prep: 15m | Cooks: 45m | Total: 1h

NUTRITION FACTS

Calories: 341 | Carbohydrates: 51.8g | Fat: 11.5g | Protein: 9g | Cholesterol: 116mg

INGREDIENTS

- 1 cup brown sugar
- 1 (1 pound) loaf French baguette, cut into 1 inch slices
- 1 teaspoon ground cinnamon
- 6 eggs, lightly beaten
- 1/2 cup butter, melted
- 1 1/2 cups milk
- 3 apples - peeled, cored and sliced
- 1 tablespoon vanilla extract
- 1/2 cup raisins
- 2 teaspoons ground cinnamon

DIRECTIONS

1. Grease a 9x13 inch baking dish. In a large bowl, mix together brown sugar and 1 teaspoon cinnamon. Mix in melted butter. Stir in apples and raisins until evenly coated. Pour into prepared pan. Arrange bread slices in an even layer over apples.
2. In the bowl, whisk together eggs, milk, vanilla and 2 teaspoons cinnamon. Pour over bread, making sure every slice is fully soaked. Cover with aluminum foil, and refrigerated overnight.
3. Preheat oven to 375 degrees F (190 degrees C). Remove dish from refrigerator while the oven is heating. Bake covered for 40 minutes. Remove cover, and bake 5 minutes. Let stand 5 minutes before serving.

ORANGE PECAN FRENCH TOAST
Servings: 12 | Prep: 20m | Cooks: 35m | Total: 1h55m

NUTRITION FACTS

Calories: 235 | Carbohydrates: 35.8g | Fat: 8.8g | Protein: 4.5g | Cholesterol: 45mg

INGREDIENTS

- 1 cup packed brown sugar
- 1/2 cup 2% milk
- 1/3 cup butter, melted
- 3 tablespoons white sugar
- 2 tablespoons light corn syrup
- 1 teaspoon ground cinnamon
- 1/3 cup chopped pecans
- 1 teaspoon vanilla extract
- 12 (3/4 inch thick) slices French bread
- 3 egg whites
- 1 teaspoon grated orange zest
- 2 eggs
- 1 cup fresh orange juice
- 1 tablespoon confectioners' sugar for dusting

DIRECTIONS

1. In a small bowl, stir together the brown sugar, melted butter, and corn syrup. Pour into a greased 9x13 inch baking dish, and spread evenly. Sprinkle pecans over the sugar mixture. Arrange the bread slices in the bottom of the dish so they are in a snug single layer.
2. In a medium bowl, whisk together the orange zest, orange juice, milk, sugar, cinnamon, vanilla, egg whites, and eggs. Pour this mixture over the bread, pressing on the bread slices to help absorb the liquid. Cover and refrigerate for at least one hour, or overnight.
3. Preheat the oven to 350 degrees F (175 degrees C). Remove the cover from the baking dish, and let stand for 20 minutes at room temperature.
4. Bake for 35 minutes in the preheated oven, until golden brown. Dust with confectioners' sugar before serving.

VERONICA'S APPLE PANCAKES

Servings: 4 | Prep: 10m | Cooks: 25m | Total: 35m

NUTRITION FACTS

Calories: 322 | Carbohydrates: 40.6g | Fat: 14.4g | Protein: 7.8g | Cholesterol: 82mg

INGREDIENTS

- 1/4 cup butter, melted
- 1 1/4 cups all-purpose flour
- 1 egg
- 1 1/4 teaspoons baking powder
- 1 cup milk

- 1/4 teaspoon ground cinnamon
- 1 cup shredded tart apple
- 1 tablespoon white sugar

DIRECTIONS

1. In a large bowl, combine butter, egg, milk and apple. In a separate bowl, sift together flour, baking powder, cinnamon and sugar. Stir flour mixture into apple mixture, just until combined.
2. Heat a lightly oiled griddle or frying pan over medium high heat. Pour or scoop the batter onto the griddle, using approximately 1/4 cup for each pancake. Brown on both sides and serve hot.

QUICHE LORRAINE

Servings: 8 | Prep: 20m | Cooks: 1h5m | Total: 1h45m

NUTRITION FACTS

Calories: 413 | Carbohydrates: 14.4g | Fat: 32.6g | Protein: 15.7g | Cholesterol: 197mg

INGREDIENTS

- 1 9-inch unbaked pie crust (see footnote for recipe link)
- 3 large eggs
- 8 slices bacon, cut into 1 inch pieces
- 2 egg yolks
- 1/2 cup chopped leeks (white and pale green parts only)
- 1 cup heavy cream
- 1/2 cup chopped onion
- 3/4 cup milk
- salt and freshly ground black pepper to taste
- 1 teaspoon chopped fresh thyme
- 1 pinch cayenne pepper, or more to taste
- 6 ounces shredded Gruyere cheese

DIRECTIONS

1. Preheat oven to 425 degrees F (220 degrees C).
2. Roll pie dough to fit a 9 inch pie plate. Place bottom crust in pie plate and chill for at least 20 minutes before baking. Line the chilled pie crust with foil and fill halfway up with dried beans, rice, or baking weights. Bake in the preheated oven for 7 minutes. Remove foil and weights and bake until golden brown, about 5 minutes.
3. Reduce oven to 325 degrees F (165 degrees C).
4. Cook bacon in a skillet over medium heat until browned and cooked through, 8 to 10 minutes. Remove from pan to drain. Blot out some of the oil from the skillet, leaving 1 to 2 teaspoons. Add leeks, onion, salt, black pepper, and cayenne pepper. Cook and stir until tender and golden brown, 5 to 7 minutes. Set aside.

5. Whisk eggs, egg yolks, cream, and milk together in a large bowl. Add thyme and stir to combine.
6. Sprinkle 2/3 of onion-leek mixture on the bottom of the baked crust. Top with 1/3 cooked bacon and 2/3 Gruyere cheese. Ladle in egg mixture carefully. Sprinkle with remaining onion-leek mixture, remaining bacon, and remaining Gruyere cheese.
7. Bake filled quiche in the preheated oven until browned and set, and no longer jiggly in the center, 40 to 45 minutes. Allow to cool slightly before serving.

BACON QUICHE TARTS

Servings: 10 | Prep: 15m | Cooks: 25m | Total: 40m

NUTRITION FACTS

Calories: 232 | Carbohydrates: 12.4g | Fat: 16.6g | Protein: 8.2g | Cholesterol: 72mg

INGREDIENTS

- 5 slices bacon
- 1/2 cup shredded Swiss cheese
- 1 (8 ounce) package cream cheese, softened
- 2 tablespoons chopped green onion
- 2 tablespoons milk
- 1 (10 ounce) can refrigerated flaky biscuit dough
- 2 eggs

DIRECTIONS

1. Preheat oven to 375 degrees F (190 degrees C). Lightly grease 10 muffin cups.
2. Place bacon in a large, deep skillet. Cook over medium high heat until crisp and evenly brown. Drain, crumble, and set aside.
3. Place the cream cheese, milk, and eggs in a medium bowl, and beat until smooth with an electric mixer set on Low. Stir in Swiss cheese and green onion, and set aside.
4. Separate dough into 10 biscuits. Press into the bottom and sides of each muffin cup, forming 1/4 inch rims. Sprinkle half of the bacon into the bottoms of the dough-lined muffin cups. Spoon about 2 tablespoons of the cream cheese mixture into each cup.
5. Bake 20 to 25 minutes in the preheated oven, until filling is set and rims of the tarts are golden brown. Sprinkle with the remaining bacon, and lightly press into the filling. Remove from pan, and serve warm.

OMELET IN A BAG

Servings: 1 | Prep: 15m | Cooks: 13m | Total: 28m

NUTRITION FACTS

Calories: 484 | Carbohydrates: 7.9g | Fat: 33.7g | Protein: 37.7g | Cholesterol: 463mg

INGREDIENTS

- 2 eggs
- 1 tablespoon chopped green bell pepper (optional)
- 2 slices ham, chopped (optional)
- 2 tablespoons chopped fresh tomato (optional)
- 1/2 cup shredded Cheddar cheese
- 1 tablespoon chunky salsa (optional)
- 1 tablespoon chopped onion (optional)
- 2 fresh mushrooms, sliced (optional)

DIRECTIONS

1. Crack the eggs into a large resealable freezer bag. Press out most of the air, and seal. Shake or squeeze to beat the eggs. Open the bag, and add the ham, cheese, onion, green pepper, tomato, salsa, and mushrooms. Squeeze out as much of the air as you can, and seal the bag.
2. Bring a large pot of water to a boil. Place up to 8 bags at a time into the boiling water. Cook for exactly 13 minutes. Open the bag, and let the omelet roll out onto a plate. The omelet should roll out easily.

GRAIN AND NUT WHOLE WHEAT PANCAKES

Servings: 6 | Prep: 10m | Cooks: 20m | Total: 30m

NUTRITION FACTS

Calories: 383 | Carbohydrates: 52.2g | Fat: 15.5g | Protein: 11.8g | Cholesterol: 37mg

INGREDIENTS

- 1 1/2 cups old-fashioned oatmeal
- 1 cup milk
- 1 1/2 cups whole wheat flour
- 1/4 cup vegetable oil
- 2 teaspoons baking soda
- 1 egg
- 1 teaspoon baking powder
- 1/3 cup sugar
- 1/2 teaspoon salt
- 3 tablespoons chopped walnuts (optional)
- 1 1/2 cups buttermilk

DIRECTIONS

1. Grind the oats in a blender or food processor until fine. In a large bowl, combine ground oats, whole wheat flour, baking soda, baking powder, and salt.
2. In another bowl, combine buttermilk, milk, oil, egg, and sugar with an electric mixer until smooth. Mix wet ingredients into dry with a few swift strokes. Stir in nuts, if desired.
3. Lightly oil a skillet or griddle, and preheat it to medium heat. Ladle 1/3 cup of the batter onto the hot skillet; cook the pancakes for 2 to 4 minutes per side, or until brown.

BANANA PEANUT BUTTER BREAD

Servings: 15 | Prep: 15m | Cooks: 1h10m | Total: 1h25m

NUTRITION FACTS

Calories: 266 | Carbohydrates: 32.1g | Fat: 13.9g | Protein: 5.5g | Cholesterol: 41mg

INGREDIENTS

- 1/2 cup butter, softened
- 2 bananas, mashed
- 1 cup white sugar
- 2 cups all-purpose flour
- 2 eggs
- 1 teaspoon baking soda
- 1/2 cup peanut butter
- 1/2 cup chopped walnuts

DIRECTIONS

1. Preheat oven to 325 degrees F (165 degrees C). Lightly grease a 5x9 inch loaf pan.
2. In a large mixing bowl, cream together butter and sugar. Add eggs; beat well. Stir in peanut butter, bananas, flour and baking soda until blended. Fold in walnuts. Pour into prepared pan.
3. Bake at 325 degrees F (165 degrees C) for 70 minutes, or until a toothpick inserted into center of the loaf comes out clean. Remove to a wire rack to cool.

FLUFFY AND DELICIOUS PANCAKES

Servings: 4 | Prep: 15m | Cooks: 10m | Total: 30m

NUTRITION FACTS

Calories: 236 | Carbohydrates: 33.5g | Fat: 8.2g | Protein: 6.4g | Cholesterol: 65mg

INGREDIENTS

- 3/4 cup milk
- 1/2 teaspoon salt
- 2 tablespoons white vinegar
- 1 egg
- 1 cup all-purpose flour
- 2 tablespoons butter, melted
- 2 tablespoons white sugar
- 1 1/2 teaspoons ground cinnamon, or as desired (optional)
- 1 teaspoon baking powder
- 1 teaspoon vanilla extract (optional)
- 1/2 teaspoon baking soda
- cooking spray

DIRECTIONS

1. Stir milk and vinegar together in a bowl; set aside to 'sour' for about 5 minutes.
2. Whisk flour, sugar, baking powder, baking soda, and salt together in a bowl. Whisk egg and butter into sour milk. Pour flour mixture into milk mixture and whisk until batter is smooth. Add cinnamon and vanilla extract to batter; mix well.
3. Heat a large skillet over medium heat and coat with cooking spray. Drop batter, 1/4 cup per pancake, onto the griddle and cook until bubbles form and the edges are dry, 3 to 4 minutes. Flip and cook until browned on the other side, 2 to 3 minutes. Repeat with remaining batter.

TENDER AND EASY BUTTERMILK WAFFLES

Servings: 6 | Prep: 15m | Cooks: 10m | Total: 25m

NUTRITION FACTS

Calories: 318 | Carbohydrates: 40.5g | Fat: 13g | Protein: 9.2g | Cholesterol: 92mg

INGREDIENTS

- 2 cups all-purpose flour
- 2 cups low-fat buttermilk
- 2 tablespoons white sugar
- 1/3 cup melted butter
- 2 teaspoons baking powder
- 2 large eggs, lightly beaten
- 1 teaspoon baking soda
- 1 teaspoon vanilla extract
- 1/2 teaspoon salt

DIRECTIONS

1. Whisk flour, sugar, baking powder, baking soda, and salt together in a bowl until evenly combined. Whisk buttermilk and butter together in a separate bowl; add eggs. Stir buttermilk mixture into flour mixture until just combined and batter is slightly lumpy; add vanilla extract.
2. Preheat a waffle iron according to manufacturer's instructions.
3. Pour enough batter into the preheated waffle iron to reach 1/2 inch from the edge. Cook according to manufacturer's instructions.

SUNSHINE TOAST

Servings: 1 | Prep: 5m | Cooks: 10m | Total: 15m

NUTRITION FACTS

Calories: 342 | Carbohydrates: 13.1g | Fat: 28.8g | Protein: 8.4g | Cholesterol: 247mg

INGREDIENTS

- 2 tablespoons butter, divided
- 1 egg
- 1 slice bread
- salt to taste

DIRECTIONS

1. Melt 1 tablespoon butter in a small skillet over medium heat.
2. Using a glass or cookie cutter, create a hole in the middle of the bread, removing the center so it is perfectly circular. Butter the bread lightly on both sides and lightly fry it on one side, and then turn it over. Crack the egg into the hole in the middle of the bread and fry quickly. Be careful that the bread does not burn. Serve warm.

LOUISIANA SWEET POTATO PANCAKES

Servings: 8 | Prep: 10m | Cooks: 15m | Total: 45m

NUTRITION FACTS

Calories: 215 | Carbohydrates: 29.2g | Fat: 8.2g | Protein: 6.2g | Cholesterol: 65mg

INGREDIENTS

- 3/4 pound sweet potatoes
- 1/2 teaspoon ground nutmeg
- 1 1/2 cups all-purpose flour
- 2 eggs, beaten
- 3 1/2 teaspoons baking powder
- 1 1/2 cups milk

- 1 teaspoon salt
- 1/4 cup butter, melted

DIRECTIONS

1. Place sweet potatoes in a medium saucepan of boiling water, and cook until tender but firm, about 15 minutes. Drain, and immediately immerse in cold water to loosen skins. Drain, remove skins, chop, and mash.
2. In a medium bowl, sift together flour, baking powder, salt, and nutmeg. Mix mashed sweet potatoes, eggs, milk and butter in a separate medium bowl. Blend sweet potato mixture into the flour mixture to form a batter.
3. Preheat a lightly greased griddle over medium-high heat. Drop batter mixture onto the prepared griddle by heaping tablespoonfuls, and cook until golden brown, turning once with a spatula when the surface begins to bubble.

MAKE AHEAD BREAKFAST CASSEROLE

Servings: 10 | Prep: 25m | Cooks: 55m | Total: 1h20m

NUTRITION FACTS

Calories: 419 | Carbohydrates: 14g | Fat: 32.4g | Protein: 18.2g | Cholesterol: 132mg

INGREDIENTS

- 2 1/2 cups seasoned croutons
- 1 (4.5 ounce) can mushrooms, drained and chopped
- 1 pound spicy pork sausage
- 1 cup shredded sharp Cheddar cheese
- 4 eggs
- 1 cup shredded Monterey Jack cheese
- 2 1/4 cups milk
- 1/4 teaspoon dry mustard
- 1 (10.75 ounce) can condensed cream of mushroom soup
- 2 sprigs fresh parsley, for garnish
- 1 (10 ounce) package frozen chopped spinach - thawed, drained and squeezed dry

DIRECTIONS

1. Spread croutons on bottom of greased 9x13 inch baking dish. Crumble sausage into medium skillet. Cook over medium heat until browned, stirring occasionally. Drain off any drippings. Spread sausage over croutons.
2. In a large bowl, whisk together eggs and milk until well blended. Stir in soup, spinach, mushrooms, cheeses and mustard. Pour egg mixture over sausage and croutons. Refrigerate overnight.
3. The next morning, preheat oven to 325 degrees F (165 degrees C).

4. Bake in preheated oven for 50 to 55 minutes or until set and lightly browned on top. Garnish with parsley sprigs and serve hot.

AMAZING MUFFIN CUPS

Servings: 12 | Prep: 20m | Cooks: 30m | Total: 50m

NUTRITION FACTS

Calories: 224 | Carbohydrates: 8.7g | Fat: 18.3g | Protein: 11.2g | Cholesterol: 114mg

INGREDIENTS

- 12 links Johnsonville Original breakfast sausage
- 6 eggs, lightly beaten
- 3 cups frozen country style shredded hash brown potatoes, thawed
- 2 cups shredded 4-cheese Mexican blend cheese
- 3 tablespoons butter, melted
- 1/4 cup chopped red bell pepper
- 1/8 teaspoon salt
- chopped fresh chives or green onion
- 1/8 teaspoon pepper

DIRECTIONS

1. Prepare sausage according to package directions. cool slightly and cut into 1/2-inch pieces; set aside.
2. In a bowl, combine hash browns, butter, salt and pepper; divide evenly into 12 greased muffin cups. Press mixture onto sides and bottom of muffin cups.
3. Bake at 400 degrees F for 12 minutes or until lightly browned. Remove from oven; divide sausage pieces into muffin cups.
4. In a bowl, combine eggs, cheese and bell pepper. Spoon mixture evenly into muffin cups. Sprinkle with chives or onion. Return to oven, bake 13-15 minutes or until set. Serve.

EASY QUICHE LORRAINE

Servings: 6 | Prep: 20m | Cooks: 35m | Total: 55m

NUTRITION FACTS

Calories: 461 | Carbohydrates: 21.1g | Fat: 33.8g | Protein: 17.9g | Cholesterol: 142mg

INGREDIENTS

- 1 recipe pastry for a 9 inch single crust pie
- 1 1/2 cups milk
- 6 slices bacon

- 1/4 teaspoon salt
- 1 onion, chopped
- 1 1/2 cups shredded Swiss cheese
- 3 eggs, beaten
- 1 tablespoon all-purpose flour

DIRECTIONS

1. Preheat oven to 450 degrees F (230 degrees C).
2. Line pastry with a double layer of aluminum foil. Bake in preheated oven for 8 minutes. Remove foil and bake for 4 to 5 minutes more, or until crust is set. Reduce oven temperature to 325 degrees F (165 degrees C).
3. Place bacon in a large, deep skillet. Cook over medium high heat until evenly brown. Remove bacon from pan, crumble and set aside. Reserve 2 tablespoons bacon grease in skillet. Cook onion in reserved drippings until tender; drain and set aside.
4. In a large bowl, mix together eggs, milk and salt. Stir in bacon and onion. In a separate bowl, toss cheese and flour together. Add cheese to egg mixture; stir well. Pour mixture into hot pastry shell.
5. Bake in preheated oven for 35 to 40 minutes, or until knife inserted into center comes out clean. If necessary, cover edges of crust with foil to prevent burning. Let quiche cool for 10 minutes before serving.

INDIVIDUAL BAKED EGGS

Servings: 1 | Prep: 10m | Cooks: 20m | Total: 30m

NUTRITION FACTS

Calories: 174 | Carbohydrates: 0.6g | Fat: 14.3g | Protein: 10.7g | Cholesterol: 212mg

INGREDIENTS

- 1 slice bacon
- 1 egg
- 1 teaspoon melted butter
- 1/4 slice Cheddar cheese

DIRECTIONS

1. Preheat oven to 350 degrees F (175 degrees C).
2. Place bacon in a large, deep skillet. Cook over medium high heat until evenly brown, but still flexible. Wrap bacon slice around the inside of a muffin cup. Place a teaspoon of butter (or bacon grease) in the bottom of muffin cup. Drop in egg.

3. Bake in preheated oven for 10 to 15 minutes. Place 1/4 slice of cheese over egg, and continue cooking until cheese is melted and egg is cooked.

BAKED OMELET ROLL

Servings: 6 | Prep: 5m | Cooks: 20m | Total: 25m

NUTRITION FACTS

Calories: 206 | Carbohydrates: 10.5g | Fat: 12.1g | Protein: 13.4g | Cholesterol: 209mg

INGREDIENTS

- 6 eggs
- 1/2 teaspoon salt
- 1 cup milk
- 1/4 teaspoon ground black pepper
- 1/2 cup all-purpose flour
- 1 cup shredded Cheddar cheese

DIRECTIONS

1. Preheat oven to 450 degrees F (230 degrees C). Lightly grease a 9x13 inch baking pan.
2. In a blender, combine eggs, milk, flour, salt and pepper; cover and process until smooth. Pour into prepared baking pan.
3. Bake in preheated oven until set, about 20 minutes. Sprinkle with cheese.
4. Carefully loosen edges of omelet from pan. Starting from the short edge of the pan, carefully roll up omelet. Place omelet seam side down on a serving plate and cut into 6 equal sized pieces.

JOSEPH'S BEST EASY BACON RECIPE

Servings: 6 | Prep: 5m | Cooks: 15m | Total: 25m | Additional: 5m

NUTRITION FACTS

Calories: 134 | Carbohydrates: 0.4g | Fat: 10.4g | Protein: 9.2g | Cholesterol: 27mg

INGREDIENTS

- 1 (16 ounce) package thick-cut bacon

DIRECTIONS

1. Line a large baking sheet with 2 sheets of aluminum foil, making sure pan is completely covered.

2. Arrange bacon strips on the prepared baking sheet, keeping at least 1/2-inch space between strips. Place pan in the cold oven.
3. Heat oven to 425 degrees F (220 degrees C). Cook bacon for 14 minutes.
4. Transfer cooked bacon to paper towel-lined plates. Let cool for 5 minutes for bacon to crisp.

TATER TOT CASSEROLE
Servings: 10 | Prep: 20m | Cooks: 35m | Total: 55m

NUTRITION FACTS

Calories: 475 | Carbohydrates: 25.8g | Fat: 36.4g | Protein: 16g | Cholesterol: 96mg

INGREDIENTS

- 1 pound ground pork breakfast sausage
- 2 eggs
- 2 cups shredded Cheddar cheese
- 2 pounds tater tots
- 2 cups milk

DIRECTIONS

1. Preheat oven to 350 degrees F (175 degrees C).
2. Place sausage in a large, deep skillet. Cook over medium-high heat until evenly brown. Drain, and spread evenly in the bottom of a 9x13 inch pan. Spread cheese over sausage.
3. In large bowl, beat together milk and eggs. Pour over cheese. (May be refrigerated overnight at this point).Top with tater tots.
4. Bake in preheated oven for 35 to 45 minutes. Cool for 5 to 10 minutes before serving.

POTATO SKILLET
Servings: 2 | Prep: 10m | Cooks: 30m | Total: 40m

NUTRITION FACTS

Calories: 485 | Carbohydrates: 16g | Fat: 37.4g | Protein: 20.8g | Cholesterol: 332mg

INGREDIENTS

- 4 slices bacon
- 1/8 teaspoon black pepper
- 2 peeled and diced potatoes
- 3 eggs, beaten

- 1/8 teaspoon garlic salt
- 1/4 cup shredded Cheddar cheese
- 1/8 teaspoon seasoning salt

DIRECTIONS

1. Place bacon in a large, deep skillet. Cook over medium-high heat until evenly brown. Remove bacon slices, reserving grease. Crumble bacon and set aside.
2. Add potatoes to bacon grease and season with garlic salt, seasoned salt and black pepper. Cook until potatoes are soft.
3. When potatoes are tender, add crumbled bacon. Pour eggs over potatoes and cook until firm. Spread with cheese and cover with lid until melted.

COUNTRY QUICHE

Servings: 8 | Prep: 20m | Cooks: 40m | Total: 1h

NUTRITION FACTS

Calories: 328 | Carbohydrates: 13.4g | Fat: 25.6g | Protein: 10.9g | Cholesterol: 122mg

INGREDIENTS

- 8 slices bacon
- 1/4 teaspoon dried thyme
- 1 small onion, chopped
- salt and pepper to taste
- 4 eggs
- 1 (9 inch) unbaked pie crust
- 2 tablespoons milk
- 1/4 cup shredded mozzarella cheese
- 2 tablespoons all-purpose flour
- 1/2 cup shredded Cheddar cheese
- 1 teaspoon dried parsley

DIRECTIONS

1. Preheat oven to 350 degrees F (175 degrees C).
2. Place bacon in a large, deep skillet. Cook over medium high heat until evenly brown. Drain (reserving 1 tablespoon of grease) crumble bacon and set aside. Heat reserved bacon grease in skillet and saute onion until soft.
3. In a large bowl, beat together eggs, milk, flour, parsley, thyme, salt and pepper. Add bacon, onion, mozzarella and cheddar cheese; mix well. Pour mixture into pie crust.

4. Bake in preheated oven for 45 minutes, or until lightly brown on top and firm in the middle. Serve warm.

PEANUT BUTTER AND BANANA FRENCH TOAST
Servings: 2 | Prep: 10m | Cooks: 5m | Total: 15m

NUTRITION FACTS

Calories: 346 | Carbohydrates: 27.6g | Fat: 23.2g | Protein: 9.8g | Cholesterol: 124mg

INGREDIENTS

- 1 egg
- 2 slices bread
- 1 dash vanilla extract
- 1 small banana, sliced
- 2 tablespoons creamy peanut butter
- 2 tablespoons butter

DIRECTIONS

1. In a small bowl, lightly beat the egg and vanilla together.
2. Spread 1 tablespoon of peanut butter on top of each slice of bread. Place the banana slices on top of one of the slices of bread. Place the other slice of bread on top of the first, to make a peanut butter and banana sandwich.
3. In a skillet or frying pan, melt the butter over medium heat. Dip the sandwich into the egg mixture and place in the heated skillet. Cook until brown on both sides. Serve hot.

SCRAMBLED EGG MUFFINS
Servings: 12 | Prep: 10m | Cooks: 20m | Total: 30m

NUTRITION FACTS

Calories: 143 | Carbohydrates: 1.6g | Fat: 1.6g | Protein: 10.2g | Cholesterol: 202mg

INGREDIENTS

- 1/2 pound bulk pork sausage
- 1/2 teaspoon salt
- 12 eggs
- 1/4 teaspoon ground black pepper
- 1/2 cup chopped onion
- 1/4 teaspoon garlic powder

- 1/2 cup chopped green bell pepper, or to taste
- 1/2 cup shredded Cheddar cheese

DIRECTIONS

1. Preheat oven to 350 degrees F (175 degrees C). Lightly grease 12 muffin cups, or line with paper muffin liners.
2. Heat a large skillet over medium-high heat and stir in sausage; cook and stir until sausage is crumbly, evenly browned, and no longer pink, 10 to 15 minutes; drain.
3. Beat eggs in a large bowl. Stir in onion, green pepper, salt, pepper, and garlic powder. Mix in sausage and Cheddar cheese. Spoon by 1/3 cupfuls into muffin cups.
4. Bake in preheated oven until a knife inserted near the center comes out clean, 20 to 25 minutes.

MONKEY BREAD

Servings: 12 | Prep: 5m | Cooks: 35m | Total: 40m

NUTRITION FACTS

Calories: 393 | Carbohydrates: 56.8g | Fat: 17g | Protein: 4.8g | Cholesterol: 1mg

INGREDIENTS

- 3 (10 ounce) packages refrigerated biscuit dough
- 1/2 cup margarine
- 3/4 cup white sugar
- 3/4 cup white sugar
- 3 tablespoons ground cinnamon

DIRECTIONS

1. Mix together 3/4 cup sugar and cinnamon.
2. Quarter the biscuits with kitchen shears. Dip shears in water after each cut to keep the biscuits from getting too sticky. Dip biscuits into sugar mixture, and place in a greased tube pan. Do this until all biscuits are used.
3. Melt butter or margarine, and mix in 3/4 cup sugar. Pour mixture over biscuits.
4. Bake in a preheated 350 degree F (175 degrees C) oven for 30 to 35 minutes.

HASH BROWN QUICHE

Servings: 6 | Prep: 15m | Cooks: 40m | Total: 55m

NUTRITION FACTS

Calories: 338 | Carbohydrates: 15.9g | Fat: 28.9g | Protein: 14.4g | Cholesterol: 127mg

INGREDIENTS

- 3 cups shredded hash brown potatoes
- 1 cup shredded Cheddar cheese
- 1/3 cup butter, melted
- 2 eggs
- seasoning salt to taste
- 1/2 cup milk
- 1 cup diced cooked ham
- salt and pepper to taste
- 1/4 cup chopped onion

DIRECTIONS

1. Preheat oven to 425 degrees F (220 degrees C).
2. Press hash browns onto the bottom and sides of a 9 inch pie dish. Drizzle with melted butter, and sprinkle with seasoning salt. Bake in preheated oven for 20 minutes, or until beginning to brown.
3. In a small bowl, combine ham, onion and shredded cheese. In a separate bowl, whisk together eggs, milk, salt, pepper, and a little seasoning salt. When crust is ready, spread ham mixture on the bottom, then cover with egg mixture.
4. Reduce oven temperature to 350 degrees F (175 degrees C.) Bake in preheated oven for 20 to 25 minutes, or until filling is puffed and golden brown.

RICH AND DELICIOUS BANANA BREAD

Servings: 10 | Prep: 10m | Cooks: 1h | Total: 1h10m

NUTRITION FACTS

Calories: 268 | Carbohydrates: 42.4g | Fat: 10.6g | Protein: 2.3g | Cholesterol: 0mg

INGREDIENTS

- 1/2 cup shortening
- 1 teaspoon baking soda
- 1 cup white sugar
- 1 teaspoon salt
- 1 1/2 cups all-purpose flour
- 3 ripe bananas

DIRECTIONS

1. Preheat oven to 325 degrees F (165 degrees C). Lightly grease an 8x4 inch loaf pan.

2. In a large bowl, cream the shortening and sugar. Sift in the flour, baking soda and salt. Blend in the mashed bananas. Pour batter into prepared pan.
3. Bake in preheated oven for 60 minutes, or until a knife inserted into center of loaf comes out clean.

FRENCH TOAST SOUFFLE
Servings: 12 | Prep: 20m | Cooks: 30m | Total: 9h20m

NUTRITION FACTS

Calories: 241 | Carbohydrates: 28.4g | Fat: 9.8g | Protein: 9.8g | Cholesterol: 142mg

INGREDIENTS

- 10 cups white bread cubes
- 2/3 cup half-and-half cream
- 1 (8 ounce) package lowfat cream cheese, softened
- 1/2 cup maple syrup
- 8 eggs
- 1/2 teaspoon vanilla extract
- 1 1/2 cups milk
- 2 tablespoons confectioners' sugar

DIRECTIONS

1. Place bread cubes in a lightly greased 9x13 inch baking pan.
2. In a large bowl, beat cream cheese with an electric mixer at medium speed until smooth. Add eggs one at a time, mixing well after each addition. Stir in milk, half and half, maple syrup, and vanilla until mixture is smooth. Pour cream cheese mixture over the bread; cover, and refrigerate overnight.
3. The next morning, remove souffle from refrigerator, and let stand at room temperature for 30 minutes. Meanwhile, preheat oven to 375 degrees F (190 degrees C).
4. Bake, uncovered, for 30 minutes in the preheated oven, or until a knife inserted in the center comes out clean. Sprinkle with confectioners' sugar, and serve warm.

LOWER FAT BANANA BREAD
Servings: 12 | Prep: 15m | Cooks: 1h | Total: 1h15m

NUTRITION FACTS

Calories: 178 | Carbohydrates: 31.2g | Fat: 4.3g | Protein: 3.9g | Cholesterol: 31mg

INGREDIENTS

- 2 eggs
- 1 tablespoon vanilla extract

- 2/3 cup white sugar
- 1 3/4 cups all-purpose flour
- 2 very ripe bananas, mashed
- 2 teaspoons baking powder
- 1/4 cup applesauce
- 1/2 teaspoon baking soda
- 1/3 cup nonfat milk
- 1/2 teaspoon salt
- 1 tablespoon vegetable oil
- 1/3 cup chopped walnuts

DIRECTIONS

1. Preheat oven to 325 degrees F (165 degrees C). Spray a bread pan with non-stick cooking spray, and lightly dust with flour.
2. In a large bowl, beat eggs and sugar in a large bowl until light and fluffy, about 5 minutes. Beat in bananas, applesauce, milk, oil and vanilla.
3. In a separate bowl, sift together flour, baking powder, baking soda and salt. Stir flour mixture into banana mixture, mixing just until blended. Fold in walnuts. Pour batter into prepared pan.
4. Bake in preheated pan until golden and a toothpick inserted into center of the loaf comes out clean, about 1 hour. Turn bread out onto a wire rack and let cool.

OVERNIGHT APPLE CINNAMON FRENCH TOAST
Servings: 15 | Prep: 20m | Cooks: 1h30m | Total: 15h

NUTRITION FACTS

Calories: 375 | Carbohydrates: 60.5g | Fat: 12.9g | Protein: 6.1g | Cholesterol: 101mg

INGREDIENTS

- 3/4 cup butter, melted
- 6 eggs
- 1 cup brown sugar
- 1 1/2 cups milk
- 1 teaspoon ground cinnamon
- 1 teaspoon vanilla extract
- 2 (21 ounce) cans apple pie filling
- 1/2 cup maple syrup
- 20 slices white bread

DIRECTIONS

1. Grease a 9x13 inch baking pan. In a small bowl, stir together the melted butter, brown sugar and cinnamon.
2. Spread the sugar mixture into the bottom of the prepared pan. Spread the apple pie filling evenly over the sugar mixture. Layer the bread slices on top of the filling, pressing down as you go. In a medium bowl, beat the eggs with the milk and vanilla. Slowly pour this mixture over the bread, making sure that it is completely absorbed. Cover the pan with aluminum foil and refrigerate overnight.
3. In the morning, preheat oven to 350 degrees F (175 degrees C).
4. Place covered pan into the oven and bake at 350 degrees F (175 degrees C) for 60 to 75 minutes. When done remove from oven and turn on broiler. Remove foil and drizzle maple syrup on top of the egg topping; broil for 2 minutes, or until the syrup begins to caramelize. Remove from the oven and let stand for 10 minutes, then cut into squares. Invert the pan onto a serving tray or baking sheet so the apple filling is on top. Serve hot.

FLUFFY CANADIAN PANCAKES
Servings: 4 | Prep: 10m | Cooks: 10m | Total: 20m

NUTRITION FACTS

Calories: 197 | Carbohydrates: 28g | Fat: 4.8g | Protein: 9.9g | Cholesterol: 159mg

INGREDIENTS

- 1 cup all-purpose flour
- 3 egg yolks
- 1 tablespoon baking powder
- 3 egg whites
- 1 cup milk

DIRECTIONS

1. In a medium bowl, combine flour and baking powder. Stir in milk and egg yolk until smooth.
2. In a large glass or metal mixing bowl, beat egg whites until stiff peaks form. Fold 1/3 of the whites into the batter, then quickly fold in remaining whites until no streaks remain.
3. Heat a lightly oiled griddle or frying pan over medium high heat. Pour or scoop the batter onto the griddle, using approximately 1/4 cup for each pancake. Cook until pancakes are golden brown on both sides; serve hot.

PUMPKIN WAFFLES WITH APPLE CIDER SYRUP
Servings: 6 | Prep: 30m | Cooks: 15m | Total: 45m

NUTRITION FACTS

Calories: 530 | Carbohydrates: 82.3g | Fat: 17.1g | Protein: 13g | Cholesterol: 161mg

INGREDIENTS

- 2 1/2 cups all-purpose flour
- 4 eggs, separated
- 4 teaspoons baking powder
- 1/4 cup butter, melted
- 2 teaspoons ground cinnamon
- 1/2 cup white sugar
- 1 teaspoon ground allspice
- 1 tablespoon cornstarch
- 1 teaspoon ground ginger
- 1 teaspoon ground cinnamon
- 1/2 teaspoon salt
- 1 cup apple cider
- 1/4 cup packed brown sugar
- 1 tablespoon lemon juice
- 1 cup canned pumpkin
- 2 tablespoons butter
- 2 cups milk

DIRECTIONS

1. Preheat a waffle iron according to manufacturer's instructions.
2. Combine the flour, baking powder, cinnamon, allspice, ginger, salt, and brown sugar in a mixing bowl. In a separate bowl, stir together the pumpkin, milk, and egg yolks. Whip the egg whites in a clean dry bowl until soft peaks form.
3. Stir the flour mixture and 1/4 cup melted butter to the pumpkin mixture, stirring just to combine. Use a whisk or rubber spatula to fold 1/3 of the egg whites into the batter, stirring gently until incorporated. Fold in the remaining egg whites. Cook waffles according to manufacturer's instructions.
4. To make the syrup, stir together the sugar, cornstarch, and cinnamon in a saucepan. Stir in the apple cider and lemon juice. Cook over medium heat until mixture begins to boil; boil until the syrup thickens. Remove from heat and stir in the 2 tablespoons of butter until melted. Serve warm.

CREAMY STRAWBERRY CREPES

Servings: 6 | Prep: 30m | Cooks: 30m | Total: 1h

NUTRITION FACTS

Calories: 557 | Carbohydrates: 49.4g | Fat: 36.8g | Protein: 9.8g | Cholesterol: 205mg

INGREDIENTS

- 3 eggs
- 1 1/4 cups sifted confectioners' sugar
- 1/2 cup milk

- 1 tablespoon lemon juice
- 1/2 cup water
- 1 teaspoon lemon zest
- 3 tablespoons butter, melted
- 1/2 teaspoon vanilla extract
- 3/4 cup all-purpose flour
- 1 cup heavy cream, whipped
- 1/2 teaspoon salt
- 4 cups sliced strawberries
- 1 (8 ounce) package cream cheese, softened

DIRECTIONS

1. Place the eggs, milk, water, melted butter, flour, and salt in the pitcher of a blender; blend until smooth.
2. Blend the cream cheese, confectioners' sugar, lemon juice, lemon zest, and vanilla with an electric mixer until smooth. Gently fold in the whipped cream.
3. Heat a lightly oiled griddle or non-stick skillet over medium heat. Pour or scoop the batter onto the griddle, using approximately 2 tablespoons for each crepe. Tip and rotate pan to spread batter as thinly as possible. Flip over when the batter is set and the edges are beginning to brown. Cook until the other side begins to brown. Stack finished crepes on a plate, cover with a damp towel and set aside.
4. To serve, fill each crepe with 1/4 cup sliced strawberries and 1/3 cup of the cream cheese filling, roll up and top with a small dollop of the cream cheese filling and more sliced strawberries.

CINNAMON GRIDDLE CAKES

Servings: 8 | Prep: 10m | Cooks: 15m | Total: 25m

NUTRITION FACTS

Calories: 330 | Carbohydrates: 59.5g | Fat: 7.9g | Protein: 5.2g | Cholesterol: 64mg

INGREDIENTS

1 1/2 cups all-purpose flour
- 2 tablespoons corn syrup
- 3 tablespoons white sugar
- 1/4 cup butter, melted
- 1/2 teaspoon salt
- 1 tablespoon vanilla extract
- 4 teaspoons baking powder
- 2 cups confectioners' sugar
- 1 tablespoon ground cinnamon
- 2 teaspoons vanilla extract

- 2 eggs, beaten
- 1 tablespoon milk
- 1 cup milk

DIRECTIONS

1. In a medium bowl, combine flour, sugar, salt, baking powder and cinnamon.
2. In a separate large bowl, beat together eggs, milk, corn syrup, butter and vanilla extract. Stir in the flour mixture.
3. Heat a lightly oiled griddle or frying pan over medium low heat. Pour or scoop the batter onto the griddle, using approximately 1/4 cup for each pancake. Brown on both sides and serve hot.
4. While pancakes are cooking, mix the icing. Combine confectioners' sugar, vanilla extract and enough milk to make a liquid frosting. Drizzle frosting on hot pancakes before serving.

IRISH SODA BREAD

Servings: 20 | Prep: 10m | Cooks: 1h | Total: 1h10m

NUTRITION FACTS

Calories: 215 | Carbohydrates: 36.8g | Fat: 5.8g | Protein: 4.5g | Cholesterol: 38mg

INGREDIENTS

- 4 cups all-purpose flour
- 1/2 teaspoon salt
- 1 cup white sugar
- 3 eggs
- 1 teaspoon baking soda
- 1 pint sour cream
- 2 teaspoons baking powder
- 1 cup raisins

DIRECTIONS

1. Preheat oven to 325 degrees F (165 degrees C). Grease two 8x4 inch loaf pans.
2. Mix the flour, sugar, baking soda, baking powder and salt. Add the eggs, sour cream and raisins and mix until just combined. Distribute batter evenly between the two pans.
3. Bake loaves at 325 degrees F (165 degrees C) for 1 hour.

PEACH FRENCH TOAST

Servings: 8 | Prep: 9h | Cooks: 45m | Total: 9h45m

NUTRITION FACTS

Calories: 362 | Carbohydrates: 51.3g | Fat: 15g | Protein: 7.2g | Cholesterol: 147mg

INGREDIENTS

- 1 cup packed brown sugar
- 12 (3/4 inch thick) slices day-old French bread
- 1/2 cup butter
- 5 eggs
- 2 tablespoons water
- 1 tablespoon vanilla extract
- 1 (29 ounce) can sliced peaches, drained
- 1 pinch ground cinnamon, or to taste

DIRECTIONS

1. In a saucepan, stir together the brown sugar, butter and water. Bring to a boil, then reduce heat to low, and simmer for 10 minutes, stirring frequently.
2. Pour the brown sugar mixture into a 9x13 inch baking dish, and tilt the dish to cover the entire bottom. Place peaches in a layer over the sugar coating, then top with slices of French bread. In a medium bowl, whisk together the eggs and vanilla. Slowly pour over the bread slices to coat evenly. Sprinkle cinnamon over the top. Cover and refrigerate for 8 hours or overnight.
3. Remove the dish from the refrigerator about 30 minutes before baking to come to room temperature. Preheat the oven to 350 degrees F (175 degrees C).
4. Bake for 25 to 30 minutes in the preheated oven, or until the bread is golden brown. Spoon out portions to serve.

BREAKFAST CASSEROLE

Servings 8 | Prep: 15m | Cooks: 1h20m | Total: 1h35m

NUTRITION FACTS

Calories: 552 | Carbohydrates: 29.9g | Fat: 38.1g | Protein: 23g | Cholesterol: 340mg

INGREDIENTS

- 6 baking potatoes
- 2 teaspoons seasoning salt
- 1 pound ground pork sausage
- 1 cup shredded Cheddar cheese
- 2 tablespoons butter
- 12 eggs, lightly beaten
- 1 onion, sliced
- salt and pepper to taste

DIRECTIONS

1. Preheat oven to 350 degrees F (175 degrees C). Lightly grease a medium baking dish.
2. Prick potatoes with a fork, place on a medium baking sheet, and bake 30 minutes, or until tender but firm. Remove from heat, cool, peel, and cube.
3. Cook and stir sausage in a medium saucepan over medium heat until evenly browned; drain.
4. Melt butter in a large saucepan over medium heat. Stir potatoes and onion into saucepan, and cook until potatoes are browned and onion is tender, about 10 minutes. Sprinkle with seasoning salt. Place potato mixture in the prepared baking dish. Cover with sausage. Sprinkle with cheese, top with eggs, and season with salt and pepper.
5. Bake 30 minutes in the preheated oven, or until eggs are fully cooked.

BABY SPINACH OMELET

Servings: 1 | Prep: 6m | Cooks: 9m | Total: 15m

NUTRITION FACTS

Calories: 186 | Carbohydrates: 2.8g | Fat: 12.3g | Protein: 16.4g | Cholesterol: 379mg

INGREDIENTS

- 2 eggs
- 1/4 teaspoon onion powder
- 1 cup torn baby spinach leaves
- 1/8 teaspoon ground nutmeg
- 1 1/2 tablespoons grated Parmesan cheese
- salt and pepper to taste

DIRECTIONS

1. In a bowl, beat the eggs, and stir in the baby spinach and Parmesan cheese. Season with onion powder, nutmeg, salt, and pepper.
2. In a small skillet coated with cooking spray over medium heat, cook the egg mixture about 3 minutes, until partially set. Flip with a spatula, and continue cooking 2 to 3 minutes. Reduce heat to low, and continue cooking 2 to 3 minutes, or to desired doneness.

HONEY NUT GRANOLA

Servings: 20 | Prep: 10m | Cooks: 20m | Total: 30m

NUTRITION FACTS

Calories: 188 | Carbohydrates: 19.9g | Fat: 11.1g | Protein: 3.7g | Cholesterol: 0mg

INGREDIENTS

- 4 cups rolled oats
- 1/3 cup canola oil
- 1 cup sliced almonds
- 1/2 cup honey
- 1 cup chopped pecans
- 1 teaspoon vanilla extract
- 1 cup raw sunflower seeds
- 1 tablespoon ground cinnamon

DIRECTIONS

1. Preheat oven to 300 degrees F (150 degrees C).
2. In a large bowl, stir oats, nuts and sunflower kernels together. In a separate bowl, mix together oil, honey, vanilla and cinnamon. Add to dry ingredients; mix well. Spread mixture onto two ungreased baking sheets.
3. Bake in preheated oven, for 10 minutes, remove from oven and stir. Return to oven and continue baking until golden, about 10 minutes. Remove from oven and let cool completely before storing.

HAM AND CHEESE QUICHE

Servings: 8 | Prep: 15m | Cooks: 55m | Total: 1h10m

NUTRITION FACTS

Calories: 283 | Carbohydrates: 14.3g | Fat: 20.1g | Protein: 11.3g | Cholesterol: 103mg

INGREDIENTS

- 2 tablespoons all-purpose flour
- 1 recipe pastry for a 9 inch single crust pie
- 1/2 teaspoon salt
- 1/2 cup chopped fresh spinach
- 1 cup half-and-half
- 1/2 cup canned mushrooms
- 3 eggs
- 1 (4.5 ounce) can ham, flaked
- 2 slices Swiss cheese
- 1/2 cup shredded Cheddar cheese

DIRECTIONS

1. Preheat oven to 350 degrees F (175 degrees C).
2. Beat together flour, salt, half-and-half and eggs in a medium bowl.

3. Place Swiss cheese flat in the pie crust. Arrange spinach evenly over Swiss cheese, then cover with mushrooms. Pour the flour and egg mixture over mushrooms. Cover with flaked ham and top with Cheddar cheese.
4. Bake in the preheated oven 45 to 55 minutes, until surface is golden brown.

STOVETOP GRANOLA

Servings: 4 | Prep: 5m | Cooks: 15m | Total: 20m

NUTRITION FACTS

Calories: 529 | Carbohydrates: 59.7g | Fat: 30.3g | Protein: 9.3g | Cholesterol: 41mg

INGREDIENTS

- 1 tablespoon olive oil
- 1/3 cup packed brown sugar
- 2 cups rolled oats
- 1/2 cup chopped almonds
- 1/3 cup butter
- 1/3 cup dried cranberries
- 2 tablespoons honey

DIRECTIONS

1. Heat the oil in a large skillet over medium-high heat. Add oats then cook and stir until starting to brown and crisp, about 5 minutes. Remove from heat and spread out on a cookie sheet to cool.
2. Melt the butter in the same pan over medium heat. Stir in the honey and brown sugar; cook, stirring constantly, until bubbly. Return the oats to the pan. Cook and stir for another 5 minutes or so. Pour out onto the cookie sheet and spread to cool.
3. Once cool, transfer to an airtight container and stir in the almonds and dried cranberries. Any additional nuts and fruit can be stirred in at this time also.

STRAWBERRY VANILLA PANCAKES

Servings: 4 | Prep: 10m | Cooks: 10m | Total: 20m

NUTRITION FACTS

Calories: 280 | Carbohydrates: 37.7g | Fat: 9.7g | Protein: 7.1g | Cholesterol: 51mg

INGREDIENTS

- 1 cup all-purpose flour
- 1 cup milk
- 2 tablespoons brown sugar

- 2 tablespoons vegetable oil
- 2 teaspoons baking powder
- 2 tablespoons vanilla extract
- 1 teaspoon salt
- 1 cup chopped fresh strawberries
- 1 egg

DIRECTIONS

1. In a medium bowl, stir together the flour, brown sugar, baking powder and salt. Pour in the milk, oil, egg and vanilla, and mix until well blended. Stir in the strawberries.
2. Heat a large skillet or griddle over medium heat, and coat with butter or cooking spray. Pour batter into desired size of pancakes. Flip with a spatula when bubbles appear in the center. Cook until golden brown on the other side.

ZUCCHINI BREAD

Servings: 24 | Prep: 20m | Cooks: 1h20m | Total: 1h40m

NUTRITION FACTS

Calories: 257 | Carbohydrates: 33.7g | Fat: 13.1g | Protein: 3g | Cholesterol: 25mg

INGREDIENTS

- 3 cups all-purpose flour
- 1 cup semisweet chocolate chips
- 3 eggs
- 1 teaspoon ground cinnamon
- 2 cups white sugar
- 1 teaspoon baking soda
- 1 cup vegetable oil
- 1/4 teaspoon baking powder
- 2 cups grated zucchini
- 1/2 cup sour cream

DIRECTIONS

1. Preheat oven to 350 degrees F (175 degrees C). Grease two 9x5-inch loaf pans.
2. Beat together eggs, sugar, and oil. Blend in the grated zucchini, and then the sour cream. Mix in the flour, baking powder, soda, and cinnamon. Stir in chocolate chips or raisins (see Cook's Note). Pour batter into prepared pans.
3. Bake in preheated oven until a tester inserted in the center of each loaf comes out clean, about 80 minutes. Cool on wire rack.

FAST AND EASY PANCAKES

Servings: 6 | Prep: 5m | Cooks: 15m | Total: 20m

NUTRITION FACTS

Calories: 323 | Carbohydrates: 61.5g | Fat: 4.4g | Protein: 9.1g | Cholesterol: 69mg

INGREDIENTS

- 2 cups milk
- 1 teaspoon vanilla extract
- 3/4 cup white sugar
- 2 cups all-purpose flour
- 2 eggs
- 1 1/2 tablespoons baking powder
- 1 teaspoon vegetable oil

DIRECTIONS

1. Place milk, sugar, eggs, oil and vanilla in the blender. Add flour and baking powder. Blend until smooth.
2. Heat a lightly oiled griddle or frying pan over medium high heat. Pour or scoop the batter onto the griddle, using approximately 1/4 cup for each pancake. Brown on both sides and serve hot.

BANANA CREPES

Servings: 6 | Prep: 5m | Cooks: 15m | Total: 20m

NUTRITION FACTS

Calories: 518 | Carbohydrates: 60.7g | Fat: 28.7g | Protein: 8g | Cholesterol: 146mg

INGREDIENTS

- 1 cup all-purpose flour
- 1/4 cup packed brown sugar
- 1/4 cup confectioners' sugar
- 1/4 teaspoon ground cinnamon
- 2 eggs
- 1/4 teaspoon ground nutmeg
- 1 cup milk
- 1/4 cup half-and-half cream
- 3 tablespoons butter, melted
- 6 bananas, halved lengthwise
- 1 teaspoon vanilla extract

- 1 1/2 cups whipped heavy cream
- 1/4 teaspoon salt
- 1 pinch ground cinnamon
- 1/4 cup butter

DIRECTIONS

1. Sift flour and powdered sugar into a mixing bowl. Add eggs, milk, butter, vanilla, and salt; beat until smooth.
2. Heat a lightly greased 6 inch skillet. Add about 3 tablespoons batter. Tilt skillet so that batter spreads to almost cover the bottom of skillet. Cook until lightly browned; turn and brown the other side. Repeat process with remaining batter, grease skillet as needed.
3. Melt 1/4 cup butter in a large skillet. Stir in brown sugar, 1/4 teaspoon cinnamon and nutmeg. Stir in cream and cook until slightly thickened. Add half the bananas at a time to skillet; cook for 2 to 3 minutes, spooning sauce over them. Remove from heat.
4. Roll a crepe around each banana half and place on serving platter. Spoon sauce over crepes. Top with whipped cream and a pinch of cinnamon.

CRAB QUICHE

Servings: 8 | Prep: 10m | Cooks: 50m | Total: 1h

NUTRITION FACTS

Calories: 346 | Carbohydrates: 16.9g | Fat: 26.1g | Protein: 11.4g | Cholesterol: 154mg

INGREDIENTS

- 1 (9 inch) deep dish frozen pie crust
- 3 dashes hot pepper sauce (e.g. Tabasco), or to taste
- 4 eggs
- 1 cup shredded Monterey Jack cheese
- 1 cup heavy cream
- 1/4 cup grated Parmesan cheese
- 1/2 teaspoon salt
- 1 (8 ounce) package imitation crabmeat, flaked
- 1/2 teaspoon black pepper
- 1 green onion, chopped

DIRECTIONS

1. Preheat the oven to 350 degrees F (175 degrees C). Bake the pie crust for about 10 minutes, until just starting to brown. Remove from the oven, and allow to cool.
2. In a large bowl, whisk together the eggs, cream, salt, pepper, and hot sauce. Stir in shredded cheese, onion and imitation crab. Pour into the pie shell.

3. Bake for 25 to 30 minutes in the preheated oven, then turn off the oven, but leave the door closed. Leave quiche in the oven for an additional 20 to 30 minutes until firm. This will give it a smoother texture.

MY-HOP PANCAKES

Servings: 8 | Prep: 15m | Cooks: 15m | Total: 1h

NUTRITION FACTS

Calories: 194 | Carbohydrates: 23.4g | Fat: 9.4g | Protein: 4.1g | Cholesterol: 29mg

INGREDIENTS

- 1 1/4 cups buttermilk
- 1 teaspoon baking soda
- 1/4 cup vegetable oil
- 1 dash salt
- 1/2 teaspoon vanilla extract
- 1 egg
- 1/4 cup white sugar
- 1 teaspoon lemon juice
- 1 1/4 cups all-purpose flour
- 1 tablespoon butter, or as needed
- 1 1/2 teaspoons baking powder

DIRECTIONS

1. Mix the buttermilk, vegetable oil, and vanilla extract in a bowl; stir in the sugar. Whisk in the flour, baking powder, baking soda, and salt, combining the batter with just a few strokes to moisten. Leave the lumps.
2. In a separate bowl, whisk the egg and lemon juice together; gently stir into the batter. Refrigerate the batter for at least 30 minutes, up to 1 hour.
3. Heat a large skillet over medium heat and grease with the butter. Pour 1/3 cup of batter per pancake into the skillet and cook until bubbles appear on the surface, about 2 minutes. Flip with spatula and brown the other side, about 2 more minutes.

PUMPKIN PANCAKES

Servings: 6 | Prep: 15m | Cooks: 45m | Total: 1h

NUTRITION FACTS

Calories: 284 | Carbohydrates: 46g | Fat: 7.9g | Protein: 7.9g | Cholesterol: 36mg

INGREDIENTS

- 2 cups all-purpose flour
- 1/2 teaspoon ground ginger
- 2 tablespoons brown sugar
- 1/2 teaspoon ground allspice
- 1 tablespoon white sugar
- 1 egg
- 2 teaspoons baking powder
- 1 1/2 cups milk
- 1 teaspoon baking soda
- 2 tablespoons vegetable oil
- 1/2 teaspoon salt
- 2 tablespoons lemon juice
- 1 cup pumpkin puree
- 2 teaspoons grated lemon zest
- 1 teaspoon ground cinnamon
- 1 teaspoon vegetable oil

DIRECTIONS

1. Combine flour, brown sugar, white sugar, baking powder, baking soda, and salt in a large mixing bowl, and whisk together for two minutes to aerate.
2. In a separate bowl, combine pumpkin puree, cinnamon, ginger, allspice, egg, milk, 2 tablespoons of vegetable oil, lemon juice, and lemon zest. Mix in the flour mixture, and stir just until moistened. (Do not overmix.)
3. Coat skillet with 1 teaspoon vegetable oil over medium heat.
4. Pour batter into skillet 1/4 cup at a time, and cook the pancakes until golden brown, about 3 minutes on each side.

WHOLE WHEAT PANCAKES

Servings: 4 | Prep: 20m | Cooks: 30m | Total: 50m

NUTRITION FACTS

Calories: 548 | Carbohydrates: 57.2g | Fat: 29.5g | Protein: 17g | Cholesterol: 163mg

INGREDIENTS

- 1 cup whole wheat flour
- 1 teaspoon salt
- 2/3 cup all-purpose flour
- 5 1/3 tablespoons unsalted butter
- 1/3 cup wheat germ

- 2 1/2 cups buttermilk
- 1 1/2 teaspoons baking powder
- 2 eggs, beaten
- 1/2 teaspoon baking soda
- 3 tablespoons unsalted butter
- 2 tablespoons brown sugar

DIRECTIONS

1. In a food processor or in a large bowl, combine the whole wheat flour, white flour, wheat germ or oats, baking powder, baking soda, brown sugar, and salt.
2. Cut the butter into small pieces with a knife, and add the butter to the flour-mixture. Mix until the mixture has a sand-like consistency.
3. Make a well in the center of the flour-butter mixture, and add the buttermilk and eggs. Stir until the liquids are fully incorporated.
4. Heat a frying pan over medium heat and grease the surface with 1 tablespoon of butter or oil. Ladle the batter onto the surface to form 4 inch pancakes. Once bubbles form on the top of the pancakes, flip them over, and cook them on the other side for about 2 minutes.

OATMEAL BANANA NUT BREAD

Servings: 12 | Prep: 20m | Cooks: 55m | Total: 1h15m

NUTRITION FACTS

Calories: 255 | Carbohydrates: 31.8g | Fat: 13g | Protein: 4.1g | Cholesterol: 31mg

INGREDIENTS

- 1/2 cup shortening
- 1 1/2 cups all-purpose flour
- 3/4 cup white sugar
- 1/2 teaspoon baking soda
- 2 eggs
- 1/2 teaspoon salt
- 1 cup mashed bananas
- 1/2 cup quick cooking oats
- 1 teaspoon vanilla extract
- 1/2 cup chopped walnuts

DIRECTIONS

1. Preheat oven to 350 degrees F (175 degrees C). Lightly grease a 9x5 inch loaf pan.

2. In a large bowl, cream together the shortening and sugar until light and fluffy. Stir in the eggs one at a time, beating well with each addition, then stir in the banana and vanilla.
3. In a separate bowl, sift together flour, baking soda and salt. Beat into creamed mixture. Stir in oats and nuts. Pour into prepared pan.
4. Bake in preheated oven for 50 to 55 minutes, or until a toothpick inserted into the center of the loaf comes out clean.

SAUSAGE BRUNCH CASSEROLE

Servings: 12 | Prep: 15m | Cooks: 15m | Total: 30m

NUTRITION FACTS

Calories: 389 | Carbohydrates: 9.3g | Fat: 31.8g | Protein: 15.1g | Cholesterol: 114mg

INGREDIENTS

- 1 1/2 pounds ground pork sausage
- 4 eggs, beaten
- 1 (8 ounce) package refrigerated crescent roll dough
- 3/4 cup milk
- 2 cups mozzarella cheese
- salt and pepper to taste

DIRECTIONS

1. Place sausage in a large, deep skillet. Cook over medium high heat until evenly brown. Drain, crumble and set aside. Preheat oven to 425 degrees F (220 degrees C).
2. Lightly grease a 9x13 inch baking pan. Lay crescent rolls flat in the bottom of the pan. Combine cooked sausage, cheese, eggs, milk, salt and pepper; pour over crescent rolls.
3. Bake in preheated oven for 15 minutes, until bubbly and rolls are baked.

BAKED OMELET SQUARES

Servings: 8 | Prep: 15m | Cooks: 30m | Total: 45m

NUTRITION FACTS

Calories: 344 | Carbohydrates: 7.2g | Fat: 27.3g | Protein: 17.9g | Cholesterol: 254mg

INGREDIENTS

- 1/4 cup butter
- chopped cooked ham (optional)

- 1 small onion, chopped
- sliced jalapeno peppers (optional)
- 1 1/2 cups shredded Cheddar cheese
- 12 eggs, scrambled
- 1 (12 ounce) can sliced mushrooms
- 1/2 cup milk
- 1 (6 ounce) can sliced black olives
- 1/2 teaspoon salt and pepper, to taste

DIRECTIONS

1. Preheat oven to 400 degrees F (205 degrees C). Grease a 9x13 inch baking dish.
2. Melt the butter in a skillet over medium heat, and cook the onion until tender.
3. Spread Cheddar cheese in the bottom of the prepared baking dish. Layer with mushrooms, olives, sauteed onion, ham, and jalapeno peppers. In a bowl, scramble eggs together with milk, and season with salt and pepper. Pour egg mixture over ingredients, but do not stir.
4. Bake, uncovered, in the preheated oven for 30 minutes, or until no longer runny in the center and slightly brown on top. Allow to cool slightly, then cut into squares and serve.

FARMER'S CASSEROLE

Servings: 6 | Prep: 25m | Cooks: 45m | Total: 1h10m

NUTRITION FACTS

Calories: 316 | Carbohydrates: 21.4g | Fat: 22.4g | Protein: 17.8g | Cholesterol: 173mg

INGREDIENTS

- 3 cups frozen hash brown potatoes
- 4 eggs, beaten
- 3/4 cup shredded pepperjack cheese
- 1 (12 fluid ounce) can evaporated milk
- 1 cup cooked ham, diced
- 1/4 teaspoon ground black pepper
- 1/4 cup chopped green onions
- 1/8 teaspoon salt

DIRECTIONS

1. Preheat oven to 350 degrees F (175 degrees C). Grease a 2 quart baking dish.
2. Arrange hash brown potatoes evenly in the bottom of the prepared dish. Sprinkle with pepperjack cheese, ham, and green onions.

3. In a medium bowl, mix the eggs, evaporated milk, pepper, and salt. Pour the egg mixture over the potato mixture in the dish. The dish may be covered and refrigerated at this point for several hours or overnight.
4. Bake for 40 to 45 minutes (or 55 to 60 minutes if made ahead and chilled) in the preheated oven, or until a knife inserted in the center comes out clean. Let stand 5 minutes before serving.

SUNDAY MORNING LEMON POPPY SEED PANCAKES

Servings: 4 | Prep: 10m | Cooks: 10m | Total: 30m

NUTRITION FACTS

Calories: 237 | Carbohydrates: 33.3g | Fat: 8.5g | Protein: 6.5g | Cholesterol: 65mg

INGREDIENTS

- 3/4 cup milk
- 2 tablespoons white sugar
- 1 tablespoon vinegar
- 1 teaspoon baking powder
- 1 tablespoon lemon juice
- 1/2 teaspoon baking soda
- 1 egg
- 1/2 teaspoon salt
- 2 tablespoons butter, melted
- 1 teaspoon poppy seeds
- 1/2 teaspoon vanilla extract
- 1 teaspoon lemon zest
- 1 cup all-purpose flour
- cooking spray

DIRECTIONS

1. Stir the milk, vinegar, and lemon juice together in a bowl; let stand 10 minutes to curdle. Whisk in egg, butter, and vanilla extract.
2. In a separate bowl, mix together the flour, sugar, baking powder, baking soda, salt, poppy seeds, and lemon zest until well combined. Pour the milk mixture into the flour mixture and whisk a few times until the batter is mostly free of lumps.
3. Heat a skillet over medium heat and spray with cooking spray. Pour 1/4 cup of batter per pancake into the skillet and cook until bubbles appear on the surface, about 2 minutes. Flip the pancakes over with a spatula and brown the other side, about 2 more minutes.

MONTE CRISTO SANDWICH - THE REAL ONE
Servings: 8 | Prep: 10m | Cooks: 5m | Total: 15m

NUTRITION FACTS

Calories: 305 | Carbohydrates: 23.7g | Fat: 17.9g | Protein: 12.2g | Cholesterol: 50mg

INGREDIENTS

- 1 quart oil for frying, or as needed
- 8 slices white bread
- 2/3 cup water
- 4 slices Swiss cheese
- 1 egg
- 4 slices turkey
- 2/3 cup all-purpose flour
- 4 slices ham
- 1 3/4 teaspoons baking powder
- 1/8 teaspoon ground black pepper
- 1/2 teaspoon salt
- 1 tablespoon confectioners' sugar for dusting

DIRECTIONS

1. Heat 5 inches of oil in a deep-fryer to 365 degrees F (180 degrees C). While oil is heating, make the batter: In a medium bowl, whisk together the egg and water. Combine the flour, baking powder, salt and pepper; whisk into the egg mixture until smooth. Set aside in the refrigerator.
2. Assemble sandwiches by placing one slice of turkey on one slice of bread, a slice of ham on another, then sandwich them with the Swiss cheese in the middle. Cut sandwiches into quarters, and secure with toothpicks.
3. Dip each sandwich quarter in the batter so that all sides are coated. Deep fry in the hot oil until golden brown on all sides. Remove toothpicks and arrange on a serving tray. Dust with confectioners' sugar just before serving.

BRUNCH ENCHILADAS
Servings: 10 | Prep: 30m | Cooks: 1h | Total: 9h30m | Additional: 8h

NUTRITION FACTS

Calories: 511 | Carbohydrates: 30.8g | Fat: 31.2g | Protein: 26.2g | Cholesterol: 173mg

INGREDIENTS

- 1 pound cooked ham, chopped

- 2 cups half-and-half cream
- 3/4 cup sliced green onions
- 1/2 cup milk
- 3/4 cup chopped green bell peppers
- 1 tablespoon all-purpose flour
- 3 cups shredded Cheddar cheese, divided
- 1/4 teaspoon garlic powder
- 10 (7 inch) flour tortillas
- 1 dash hot pepper sauce
- 5 eggs, beaten

DIRECTIONS

1. Place ham in food processor, and pulse until finely ground. Mix together ham, green onions, and green peppers. Spoon 1/3 cup of the ham mixture and 3 tablespoons shredded cheese onto each tortilla, then roll up. Carefully place filled tortillas, seam side down, in a greased 9x13 baking dish.
2. In a medium bowl, mix together eggs, cream, and milk, flour, garlic powder, and hot pepper sauce. Pour egg mixture over tortillas. Cover, and refrigerate overnight.
3. The next morning, preheat oven to 350 degrees F (175 degrees C).
4. Bake, uncovered, in preheated oven for 50 to 60 minutes, or until set. Sprinkle casserole with remaining 1 cup shredded cheese. Bake about 3 minutes more, or until cheese melts. Let stand a least 10 minutes before serving.

HOME-FRIED POTATOES

Servings: 4 | Prep: 20m | Cooks: 25m | Total: 45m

NUTRITION FACTS

Calories: 262 | Carbohydrates: 38.3g | Fat: 10.6g | Protein: 4.7g | Cholesterol: 0mg

INGREDIENTS

- 4 red potatoes
- 1 teaspoon salt
- 1 tablespoon olive oil
- 3/4 teaspoon paprika
- 1 onion, chopped
- 1/4 teaspoon ground black pepper
- 1 green bell pepper, seeded and chopped
- 1/4 cup chopped fresh parsley
- 2 tablespoons olive oil

DIRECTIONS

1. Bring a large pot of salted water to a boil. Add potatoes and cook until tender but still firm, about 15 minutes. Drain, cool cut into 1/2 inch cubes.
2. In a large skillet, heat 1 tablespoon olive oil over medium high heat. Add onion and green pepper. Cook, stirring often, until soft; about 5 minutes. Transfer to a plate and set aside.
3. Pour remaining 2 tablespoons of oil into the skillet and turn heat to medium-high. Add potato cubes, salt, paprika and black pepper. Cook, stirring occasionally, until potatoes are browned; about 10 minutes. Stir in the onions, green peppers and parsley and cook for another minute. Serve hot.

BLUEBERRY FRENCH TOAST
Servings: 12 | Prep: 30m | Cooks: 1h | Total: 15h

NUTRITION FACTS

Calories: 374 | Carbohydrates: 49 g | Fat: 14.7g | Protein: 12.6g | Cholesterol: 212mg

INGREDIENTS

- 1 (1 pound) loaf Italian bread, cut into 1-inch cubes
- 1 cup white sugar
- 1 (8 ounce) package cream cheese, diced
- 2 tablespoons cornstarch
- 1 cup blueberries
- 1 cup water
- 12 eggs
- 1 cup blueberries
- 2 cups milk
- 1 tablespoon butter
- 1/3 cup maple syrup

DIRECTIONS

1. Place half of the bread cubes in a lightly greased 9x13 inch baking pan. Sprinkle cream cheese on top of bread cubes. Top with 1 cup blueberries and remaining bread. In a large bowl, beat together eggs, milk and maple syrup. Pour egg mixture over bread. Cover pan and refrigerate overnight.
2. The next morning, remove pan from refrigerator 30 minutes before baking. Preheat oven to 350 degrees F (175 degrees C).
3. Cover pan with aluminum foil and bake in preheated oven for 30 minutes. Uncover pan and bake for an additional 30 minutes, until golden brown and center is set.
4. To make Sauce: In a saucepan, combine sugar and cornstarch, add water. Boil over medium heat for 3 minutes, stirring constantly. Stir in blueberries and reduce heat. Simmer 8 to 10 minutes, or until the berries have burst. Stir in butter until melted. Serve the sauce over squares of french toast.

CLASSIC HASH BROWNS

Servings: 2 | Prep: 10m | Cooks: 10m | Total: 20m

NUTRITION FACTS

Calories: 334 | Carbohydrates: 37.5g | Fat: 19.4g | Protein: 4.4g | Cholesterol: 49mg

INGREDIENTS

- 2 russet potatoes, peeled
- 1 pinch cayenne pepper, or to taste
- 3 tablespoons clarified butter
- 1 pinch paprika, or to taste
- salt and ground black pepper to taste

DIRECTIONS

1. Shred potatoes into a large bowl filled with cold water. Stir until water is cloudy, drain, and cover potatoes again with fresh cold water. Stir again to dissolve excess starch. Drain potatoes well, pat dry with paper towels, and squeeze out any excess moisture.
2. Heat clarified butter in a large non-stick pan over medium heat. Sprinkle shredded potatoes into the hot butter and season with salt, black pepper, cayenne pepper, and paprika.
3. Cook potatoes until a brown crust forms on the bottom, about 5 minutes. Continue to cook and stir until potatoes are browned all over, about 5 more minutes.

BAKED PUMPKIN BREAD

Servings: 12 | Prep: 10m | Cooks: 1h | Total: 1h10m

NUTRITION FACTS

Calories: 162 | Carbohydrates: 32.3g | Fat: 2.7g | Protein: 2.8g | Cholesterol: 21mg

INGREDIENTS

- 1 1/2 cups all-purpose flour
- 1 cup solid pack pumpkin puree
- 1 1/4 teaspoons baking soda
- 1 cup packed brown sugar
- 1 teaspoon salt
- 1/2 cup buttermilk
- 1 teaspoon ground cinnamon
- 1 egg
- 1/2 teaspoon ground nutmeg

- 2 tablespoons butter, softened

DIRECTIONS

1. Preheat oven to 350 degrees F (175 degrees C).
2. Sift the flour, baking soda, salt, cinnamon and nutmeg into a large bowl. Mix in the pumpkin, brown sugar, buttermilk, egg and butter until well blended. Pour into a 9x5 inch loaf pan and smooth the top.
3. Bake for 1 hour in the preheated oven, or until a toothpick inserted into the center comes out clean.

EMMA'S BELGIAN WAFFLES

Servings: 6 | Prep: 10m | Cooks: 20m | Total: 1h10m

NUTRITION FACTS

Calories: 445 | Carbohydrates: 57.2g | Fat: 19g | Protein: 10.6g | Cholesterol: 115mg

INGREDIENTS

- 2 egg yolks
- 1 teaspoon salt
- 5 tablespoons white sugar
- 2 3/4 cups self-rising flour
- 1 1/2 teaspoons vanilla extract
- 2 cups warm milk
- 1/2 cup butter, melted
- 2 egg whites

DIRECTIONS

1. In a large bowl, beat together egg yolks and sugar. Beat in vanilla extract, butter and salt. Alternately mix in flour and milk until blended well.
2. In a separate bowl, beat egg whites until they have formed soft peaks. Fold egg whites into batter and let stand for 40 minutes.
3. Spray preheated waffle iron with non-stick cooking spray. Pour mix onto hot waffle iron. Cook until golden brown and fluffy.

BANANA BREAD

Servings: 12 | Prep: 15m | Cooks: 1h | Total: 1h15m

NUTRITION FACTS

Calories: 215 | Carbohydrates: 30.3g | Fat: 9.4g | Protein: 3.9g | Cholesterol: 45mg

INGREDIENTS

- 1 3/4 cups all-purpose flour
- 1/3 cup butter, softened
- 2 teaspoons baking powder
- 2 eggs
- 1/4 teaspoon baking soda
- 1 cup mashed banana
- 1/2 teaspoon salt
- 1/2 cup chopped walnuts
- 2/3 cup white sugar

DIRECTIONS

1. Grease an 8x4 inch loaf pan. Preheat oven to 350 degrees F (175 degrees C).
2. In a large mixing bowl, sift together flour, baking powder, baking soda, salt, and sugar. Add butter, eggs, nuts, and mashed banana. Beat until well blended.
3. Pour batter into prepared pan and bake about 1 hour, or until a toothpick inserted in the center of the loaf comes out clean.

CHAKCHOUKA (SHAKSHOUKA)

Servings: 4 | Prep: 20m | Cooks: 20m | Total: 40m

NUTRITION FACTS

Calories: 209 | Carbohydrates: 12.9g | Fat: 15g | Protein: 7.8g | Cholesterol: 164mg

INGREDIENTS

- 3 tablespoons olive oil
- 1 teaspoon ground cumin
- 1 1/3 cups chopped onion
- 1 teaspoon paprika
- 1 cup thinly sliced bell peppers, any color
- 1 teaspoon salt
- 2 cloves garlic, minced, or to taste
- 1 hot chile pepper, seeded and finely chopped, or to taste
- 2 1/2 cups chopped tomatoes
- 4 eggs

DIRECTIONS

1. Heat the olive oil in a skillet over medium heat. Stir in the onion, bell peppers, and garlic; cook and stir until the vegetables have softened and the onion has turned translucent, about 5 minutes.
2. Combine the tomatoes, cumin, paprika, salt, and chile pepper into a bowl and mix briefly. Pour the tomato mixture into the skillet, and stir to combine.
3. Simmer, uncovered, until the tomato juices have cooked off, about 10 minutes. Make four indentations in the tomato mixture for the eggs. Crack the eggs into the indentations. Cover the skillet and let the eggs cook until they're firm but not dry, about 5 minutes.

BAKED EGGS

Servings: 1 | Prep: 10m | Cooks: 10m | Total: 20m

NUTRITION FACTS

Calories: 560 | Carbohydrates: 39.2g | Fat: 35.9g | Protein: 20.6g | Cholesterol: 418mg

INGREDIENTS

- 1/3 cup marinara sauce
- 1 tablespoon finely shredded Parmigiano-Reggiano cheese
- 1/2 teaspoon red pepper flakes
- 2 teaspoons olive oil
- salt and freshly ground black pepper to taste
- 2 tablespoons heavy whipping cream
- 1 1/2 teaspoons chopped fresh flat-leaf parsley
- 2 slices toast
- 2 eggs

DIRECTIONS

1. Preheat oven to 400 degrees F (200 degrees C).
2. Spoon marinara sauce into the bottom of a small baking dish, about 1/4 inch high. Sprinkle with red pepper flakes, salt, black pepper, and parsley. Make a narrow well in the center of the sauce for the eggs.
3. Crack each egg into a ramekin, then pour into the baking dish over the marinara sauce.
4. Sprinkle with Parmigiano-Reggiano cheese, olive oil, and cream. Season with salt and black pepper to taste.
5. Bake in the preheated oven until yolks are just set, 10 to 12 minutes. Serve with toast.

QUICK ALMOND FLOUR PANCAKES

Servings: 4 | Prep: 10m | Cooks: 10m | Total: 20m

NUTRITION FACTS

Calories: 240 | Carbohydrates: 10.1g | Fat: 19g | Protein: 9.7g | Cholesterol: 93mg

INGREDIENTS

- 1 cup almond flour
- 1 tablespoon maple syrup
- 1/4 cup water
- 1/4 teaspoon salt
- 2 eggs
- 1 teaspoon oil, or as needed

DIRECTIONS

1. Whisk almond flour, water, eggs, maple syrup, and salt together in a bowl until batter is smooth.
2. Heat oil in a skillet over medium heat; drop batter by large spoonfuls onto the griddle, and cook until bubbles form and the edges are dry, 3 to 5 minutes. Flip, and cook until browned on the other side, 3 to 5 minutes. Repeat with remaining batter.

COUNTRY STYLE FRIED POTATOES

Servings: 6 | Prep: 10m | Cooks: 15m | Total: 25m

NUTRITION FACTS

Calories: 326 | Carbohydrates: 52.1g | Fat: 11.7g | Protein: 4.8g | Cholesterol: 0mg

INGREDIENTS

- 1/3 cup shortening
- 1/2 teaspoon ground black pepper
- 6 large potatoes, peeled and cubed
- 1/2 teaspoon garlic powder
- 1 teaspoon salt
- 1/2 teaspoon paprika

DIRECTIONS

1. In a large cast iron skillet, heat shortening over medium-high heat. Add potatoes and cook, stirring occasionally, until potatoes are golden brown. Season with salt, pepper, garlic powder and paprika. Serve hot.

KIELBASA AND POTATO BAKE

Servings: 8 | Prep: 15m | Cooks: 1h30m | Total: 1h45m

NUTRITION FACTS

Calories: 352 | Carbohydrates: 33.3g | Fat: 19.1g | Protein: 12g | Cholesterol: 42mg

INGREDIENTS

- 1 (10.75 ounce) can condensed cream of mushroom soup
- 1/2 teaspoon ground black pepper
- 2 cups milk
- 1 pound kielbasa sausage, sliced thin
- 1 tablespoon minced garlic
- 4 large russet potatoes, peeled and cubed
- 1 teaspoon salt

DIRECTIONS

1. Preheat oven to 375 degrees F (190 degrees C).
2. In a large mixing bowl, mix together soup, milk, garlic, salt, and pepper. Stir in potatoes and kielbasa. Spoon into a 7x11 inch casserole dish.
3. Place casserole on a baking sheet, and bake in the preheated oven for 90 minutes, or until potatoes are tender.

DOMINICAN STYLE OATMEAL

Servings: 2 | Prep: 10m | Cooks: 5m | Total: 15m

NUTRITION FACTS

Calories: 220 | Carbohydrates: 35.3g | Fat: 5.1g | Protein: 8.7g | Cholesterol: 15mg

INGREDIENTS

- 1 1/2 cups milk
- 1 pinch ground nutmeg
- 1/2 cup quick cooking oats
- 1 pinch salt
- 2 tablespoons white sugar
- 1/4 teaspoon lemon zest (optional)
- 1/4 teaspoon ground cinnamon

DIRECTIONS

1. Combine milk, oats, sugar, cinnamon, nutmeg, and salt in a saucepan. Add lemon peel, if using. Bring to a boil, stirring constantly for 2 minutes.

SHRIMP AND GRITS

Servings: 4 | Prep: 25m | Cooks: 30m | Total: 55m

NUTRITION FACTS

Calories: 434 | Carbohydrates: 33.2g | Fat: 19.5g | Protein: 30.1g | Cholesterol: 226mg

INGREDIENTS

- 1/4 cup water
- 1 pound shrimp, peeled and deveined
- 2 tablespoons heavy whipping cream
- 1/2 teaspoon Cajun seasoning
- 2 teaspoons lemon juice
- 1/2 teaspoon salt, or to taste
- 1 dash Worcestershire sauce
- 1/4 teaspoon ground black pepper
- 4 cups water
- 1 pinch cayenne pepper
- 2 tablespoons butter
- 1 tablespoon minced jalapeno pepper
- 1 teaspoon salt
- 2 tablespoons minced green onion
- 1 cup white grits
- 3 cloves garlic, minced
- 1/2 cup shredded white Cheddar cheese
- 1 tablespoon chopped fresh parsley
- 1/4 cup water

DIRECTIONS

1. Place bacon in a large skillet and cook over medium-high heat, turning occasionally, until almost crisp, 5 to 7 minutes. Remove from heat and transfer bacon to a dish, leaving drippings in the skillet.
2. Whisk 1/4 cup water, cream, lemon juice, and Worcestershire sauce together in a bowl.
3. Stir 4 cups water, butter, and 1 teaspoon salt together in a pot; bring to a boil. Whisk grits into pot, bring to a simmer, reduce heat to low, and cook until grits are creamy, 20 to 25 minutes. Remove from heat and stir white Cheddar cheese into grits.
4. Place shrimp in a large bowl and season with Cajun seasoning, 1/2 teaspoon salt, black pepper, and a pinch of cayenne pepper.
5. Heat skillet with bacon drippings over high heat. Cook shrimp in hot bacon fat in a single layer for 1 minute. Turn shrimp and add jalapeno; cook until fragrant, about 30 seconds. Stir cream mixture, bacon, green onion, and garlic to shrimp mixture; cook and stir, adding water as necessary to thin the sauce, until shrimp are cooked through, 3 to 4 minutes. Remove from heat and stir in parsley.
6. Ladle grits into a bowl and top with shrimp and sauce.

BREAKFAST PIZZA

Servings: 8 | Prep: 15m | Cooks: 25m | Total: 40m

NUTRITION FACTS

Calories: 342 | Carbohydrates: 15.9g | Fat: 22.1g | Protein: 20.8g | Cholesterol: 165mg

INGREDIENTS

- 1 pound ground breakfast sausage
- 1/4 cup milk
- 1 (8 ounce) package refrigerated crescent rolls
- 1/2 teaspoon salt
- 1 cup frozen hash brown potatoes, thawed
- 1/8 teaspoon ground black pepper
- 1 cup shredded Cheddar cheese
- 1/4 cup grated Parmesan cheese
- 5 eggs

DIRECTIONS

1. Place sausage in a large, deep skillet. Cook over medium high heat until evenly brown. Drain, crumble and set aside. Preheat oven to 375 degrees F (190 degrees C).
2. Brown sausage and drain. Separate crescent roll dough into 8 triangles. Place in an ungreased 12 inch pizza pan with points toward the center. Press together to form a crust. Bottom of crust should be sealed and outside edge should be slightly raised. Spoon sausage over crust. Sprinkle with hash browns and top with cheddar cheese.
3. Beat together eggs, milk, salt and pepper; pour over crust. Sprinkle with parmesan cheese.
4. Bake in preheated oven until eggs are set, about 25 to 30 minutes.

HAM AND CHEESE BREAKFAST QUICHE

Servings: 5 | Prep: 20m | Cooks: 55m | Total: 1h15m

NUTRITION FACTS

Calories: 461 | Carbohydrates: 25.2g | Fat: 32.9g | Protein: 17.6g | Cholesterol: 176mg

INGREDIENTS

- 2 (12 ounce) packages frozen hash brown potatoes
- 1 cup shredded Monterey Jack cheese
- 1/3 cup butter, melted
- 2 eggs

- 1 cup cooked diced ham
- 1/2 cup heavy whipping cream

DIRECTIONS

1. Preheat oven to 425 degrees F (220 degrees C).
2. Squeeze any excess moisture from the potatoes and combine them with the melted butter or margarine in a small bowl. Press this mixture into the bottom and sides of an ungreased 10 inch pie pan.
3. Bake at 425 degrees F (220 degrees C) for 25 minutes.
4. Remove pan from oven and arrange the ham and cheese evenly over the potatoes. In a separate small bowl, beat together the eggs and the cream. Pour this over the ham and cheese.
5. Return pan to oven and bake for 425 degrees F (220 degrees C) for 30 minutes, or until the custard has completely set.

PUMPKIN SPICED LATTE

Servings: 3 | Prep: 15m | Cooks: 3m | Total: 18m

NUTRITION FACTS

Calories: 158 | Carbohydrates: 18.3g | Fat: 5.6g | Protein: 8.3g | Cholesterol: 22mg

INGREDIENTS

- 3 cups hot whole milk
- 6 ounces double-strength brewed coffee
- 4 teaspoons white sugar
- 3 tablespoons sweetened whipped cream
- 1/2 teaspoon vanilla extract
- 3 pinches pumpkin pie spice
- 1/2 teaspoon pumpkin pie spice

DIRECTIONS

1. Combine the hot milk, sugar, vanilla extract, and pumpkin pie spice in a blender; blend until frothy. Pour the mixture into 3 coffee mugs to about 2/3 full. Pour 2 ounces coffee into each mug. Garnish each mug with whipped topping and pumpkin pie spice.

CREAMED EGGS ON TOAST

Servings: 6 | Prep: 20m | Cooks: 5m | Total: 25m

NUTRITION FACTS

Calories: 391 | Carbohydrates: 27.6g | Fat: 21.7g | Protein: 19.8g | Cholesterol: 454mg

INGREDIENTS

- 12 hard-cooked eggs, peeled
- 1 tablespoon chicken bouillon granules
- 1/4 cup butter
- 6 slices white bread, lightly toasted
- 1/2 cup all-purpose flour
- salt and white pepper to taste
- 3 cups milk

DIRECTIONS

1. Separate the egg whites from the egg yolks. Place the egg yolks into a bowl and mash with a fork. Chop the egg whites into small pieces and set aside.
2. Melt the butter in a saucepan set over medium heat. Stir in flour until smooth. Gradually mix in the milk and chicken bouillon so that no lumps form and stir constantly until the mixture comes to a boil. Add the egg yolks and mix until dissolved. Stir in egg whites. Serve over toast and season with salt and white pepper.

CRAB AND SWISS QUICHE

Servings: 8 | Prep: 15m | Cooks: 40m | Total: 55m

NUTRITION FACTS

Calories: 343 | Carbohydrates: 17.2g | Fat: 25.7g | Protein: 11.2g | Cholesterol: 77mg

INGREDIENTS

- 2 egg, lightly beaten
- 1/2 pound imitation crab meat, flaked
- 1/2 cup milk
- 1 1/2 cups shredded Swiss cheese
- 1/2 cup mayonnaise
- 1 (9 inch) unbaked pie crust
- 1 teaspoon cornstarch

DIRECTIONS

1. Preheat oven to 350 degrees F (175 degrees C).

2. In a medium bowl, mix together eggs, milk, mayonnaise and cornstarch. Mix in the imitation crab and Swiss cheese. Pour into pie shell.
3. Bake in preheated oven until a knife inserted into center of the quiche comes out clean, about 30 to 40 minutes.

EGG AND HASH BROWN PIE

Servings: 4 | Prep: 15m | Cooks: 45m | Total: 1h5m | Additional: 5m

NUTRITION FACTS

Calories: 223 | Carbohydrates: 12g | Fat: 17g | Protein: 13.5g | Cholesterol: 147mg

INGREDIENTS

- 6 slices bacon
- 3 cups frozen hash brown potatoes, thawed
- 5 eggs
- 1/3 cup chopped green onions
- 1/2 cup milk
- 1 1/2 cups shredded Cheddar cheese, divided

DIRECTIONS

1. Place bacon in a large, deep skillet. Cook over medium high heat until evenly brown. Drain, crumble, and set aside.
2. Preheat oven to 350 degrees F (175 degrees C). Lightly grease a 7x11 inch baking dish.
3. In a large bowl, beat together the eggs and milk. Stir in the bacon, hash browns, green onions, and 1 cup shredded Cheddar cheese. Pour into the prepared baking dish.
4. Bake in the preheated oven 25 to 35 minutes, or until a knife inserted in the center comes out clean. Sprinkle the remaining Cheddar cheese on top, and continue baking for 3 to 4 minutes, or until the cheese is melted. Remove from oven, and let sit 5 minutes before serving.

AUTHENTIC MEXICAN BREAKFAST TACOS

Servings: 4 | Prep: 5m | Cooks: 10m | Total: 15m

NUTRITION FACTS

Calories: 537 | Carbohydrates: 27.7g | Fat: 34.1g | Protein: 30.6g | Cholesterol: 343mg

INGREDIENTS

- 6 ounces chorizo sausage

- 1/2 teaspoon salt
- 8 (6 inch) corn tortillas
- 1 cup shredded Monterey Jack cheese
- 6 eggs
- 1 dash hot pepper sauce (e.g. Tabasco), or to taste
- 1/4 cup milk
- 1/2 cup salsa
- 1/2 teaspoon pepper

DIRECTIONS

1. Crumble the sausage into a skillet over medium-high heat. Cook and stir until evenly brown. Set aside.
2. Heat one skillet over medium heat, and heat another skillet over high heat. The skillet over high heat is for warming tortillas. In a medium bowl, whisk together the eggs, milk, salt and pepper. Spray the medium heat skillet with some cooking spray, and pour in the eggs. Cook and stir until almost firm. Add the sausage, and continue cooking and stirring until firm.
3. Meanwhile, warm tortillas for about 45 seconds per side in the other skillet, so they are hot and crispy on the edges, but still pliable.
4. Sprinkle a little shredded cheese onto each tortilla while it is still hot. Top with some of the scrambled egg and sausage, then add hot pepper sauce and salsa to your liking.

PEAR BREAD

Servings: 20 | Prep: 10m | Cooks: 1h | Total: 1h20m | Additional: 10m

NUTRITION FACTS

Calories: 304 | Carbohydrates: 38.5g | Fat: 15.8g | Protein: 3.5g | Cholesterol: 28mg

INGREDIENTS

- 1 cup vegetable oil
- 3 cups all-purpose flour
- 2 cups granulated sugar
- 1 teaspoon baking soda
- 3 eggs
- 1 teaspoon baking powder
- 2 1/2 cups pears - peeled, cored and chopped
- 1 teaspoon salt
- 1 cup chopped pecans
- 1 teaspoon ground cinnamon
- 2 teaspoons vanilla extract
- 1/2 teaspoon ground nutmeg

DIRECTIONS

1. Preheat oven to 350 degrees F (175 degrees C). Lightly grease two 8x4 inch loaf pans.
2. In large mixing bowl combine oil, sugar and eggs, beat well. Stir in pears, pecans and vanilla. In another bowl, combine flour, baking soda, baking powder, salt, cinnamon and nutmeg. Stir dry ingredients into the pear mixture; mix well. Pour batter into prepared loaf pans.
3. Bake in preheated oven for 60 minutes, until a toothpick inserted into center of a loaf comes out clean. Allow loaves to cool in pans for 10 minutes before moving to a wire rack to cool completely.

QUICK AND EASY MONKEY BREAD
Servings: 12 | Prep: 10m | Cooks: 30m | Total: 40m

NUTRITION FACTS

Calories: 389 | Carbohydrates: 59.6g | Fat: 14.5g | Protein: 6.9g | Cholesterol: 23mg

INGREDIENTS

- 24 ounces frozen dinner roll dough
- 2 teaspoons ground cinnamon
- 1 cup packed brown sugar
- 1/2 cup chopped walnuts
- 1 (3.4 ounce) package instant butterscotch pudding mix
- 1/2 cup melted butter
- 1/4 cup white sugar

DIRECTIONS

1. The night or several hours before, grease and flour a 9 or 10 inch tube pan. Mix brown sugar and pudding mix together. Mix white sugar and cinnamon together. Place frozen dinner rolls in pan a layer at a time. Sprinkle brown sugar and pudding mix over first layer of rolls. Sprinkle sugar and cinnamon mixture over the brown sugar and pudding mixture. Spread half the nuts and melted butter over first layer. Repeat with the next layer.
2. Place on counter over night. Do not cover. Next morning bake in a preheated 350 degrees F (175 degrees C) oven for 30 minutes. Let stand a few minutes and turn pan over onto serving platter.

OVERNIGHT FRENCH TOAST
Servings: 5 | Prep: 20m | Cooks: 45m | Total: 1h5m

NUTRITION FACTS

Calories: 723 | Carbohydrates: 104g | Fat: 26.5g | Protein: 19.5g | Cholesterol: 241mg

INGREDIENTS

- 2 tablespoons corn syrup
- 5 eggs
- 1/2 cup butter
- 1 1/2 cups milk
- 1 cup packed brown sugar
- 1 teaspoon vanilla extract
- 1 (1 pound) loaf French bread, sliced
- 1/4 teaspoon salt

DIRECTIONS

1. Combine the corn syrup, butter, and brown sugar in a small saucepan and simmer until the sugar has melted. Pour this mixture over the bottom of a greased 9x13 inch casserole dish.
2. Place the bread slices over the sugar-butter mixture in the dish. In a bowl, beat together the eggs, milk, vanilla, and salt; pour this mixture over the bread. Cover the dish and let it stand in the refrigerator overnight.
3. The next morning, preheat oven to 350 degrees F (175 degrees C).
4. Uncover the pan and bake for 45 minutes. Serve while hot or warm or the French toast will harden in the pan. It can be reheated.

SAUSAGE CRESCENT ROLLS

Servings: 20 | Prep: 25m | Cooks: 20m | Total: 50m | Additional: 5m

NUTRITION FACTS

Calories: 225 | Carbohydrates: 9.4g | Fat: 18g | Protein: 5.4g | Cholesterol: 28mg

INGREDIENTS

- 1 pound fresh, ground spicy pork sausage
- 1 egg white, lightly beaten
- 1 (8 ounce) package cream cheese
- 1 tablespoon poppy seeds
- 2 (8 ounce) packages refrigerated crescent rolls

DIRECTIONS

1. Preheat oven to 350 degrees F (175 degrees C).
2. In a medium skillet, lightly brown sausage and drain. While sausage is still hot, add cream cheese and stir until cheese is melted and mixture is creamy. Cool completely.

3. Separate crescent rolls and arrange into two rectangles. Form log of sausage mixture lengthwise down center of each rectangle. Fold over the long sides of pastry to cover sausage log. Place on ungreased cookie sheet, seam down. Brush with egg white and sprinkle with poppy seeds.
4. Bake 20 minutes until crust is golden. When completely cooled, slice into one and one-half inch slices.

EASY SWEDISH PANCAKES
Servings: 4 | Prep: 10m | Cooks: 10m | Total: 20m

NUTRITION FACTS

Calories: 252 | Carbohydrates: 21.1g | Fat: 13.3g | Protein: 12g | Cholesterol: 211mg

INGREDIENTS

- 4 eggs
- 1 tablespoon sugar
- 2 cups milk
- 1 pinch salt
- 1/2 cup all-purpose flour
- 2 tablespoons melted butter

DIRECTIONS

1. In a large bowl, beat eggs with a wire whisk. Mix in milk, flour, sugar, salt, and melted butter.
2. Preheat a non-stick electric skillet to medium heat. Pour a thin layer of batter on skillet, and spread to edges. Cook until top surface appears dry. Cut into 2 or 4 sections, and flip with a spatula. Cook for another 2 minutes, or until golden brown. Roll each pancake up, and serve.

EXTRA-YUMMY FLUFFY PANCAKES
Servings: 6 | Prep: 10m | Cooks: 40m | Total: 55m

NUTRITION FACTS

Calories: 218 | Carbohydrates: 27g | Fat: 9.7g | Protein: 5.6g | Cholesterol: 35mg

INGREDIENTS

- 1 1/4 cups all-purpose flour
- 1 1/3 cups milk
- 1 1/2 tablespoons white sugar
- 1 egg, lightly beaten
- 1 tablespoon baking powder

- 3 tablespoons vegetable oil
- 1 tablespoon ground cinnamon
- 3/4 teaspoon vanilla extract
- 3/4 teaspoon salt
- 1 teaspoon vegetable oil, or as needed

DIRECTIONS

1. Whisk together flour, sugar, baking powder, cinnamon, and salt in a bowl. Whisk in the milk, egg, 3 tablespoons vegetable oil, and vanilla extract until only a few lumps remain. Let the batter stand for 5 full minutes for extra fluffiness.
2. Heat a skillet or griddle over medium heat, and brush with 1 teaspoon vegetable oil. When the oil shimmers, slowly pour about 1/4 cup of batter into the hot pan. Cook until bottom is browned, about 2 minutes, then flip and cook until the center of the pancake is set and the other side is browned, about 2 more minutes. Keep warm until serving.

DELICIOUS GLUTEN-FREE PANCAKES

Servings: 10 | Prep: 20m | Cooks: 15m | Total: 35m

NUTRITION FACTS

Calories: 147 | Carbohydrates: 20.4g | Fat: 5.8g | Protein: 3.1g | Cholesterol: 29mg

INGREDIENTS

- 1 cup rice flour
- 1/2 teaspoon baking soda
- 3 tablespoons tapioca flour
- 1/2 teaspoon salt
- 1/3 cup potato starch
- 1/2 teaspoon xanthan gum
- 4 tablespoons dry buttermilk powder
- 2 eggs
- 1 packet sugar substitute
- 3 tablespoons canola oil
- 1 1/2 teaspoons baking powder
- 2 cups water

DIRECTIONS

1. In a bowl, mix or sift together the rice flour, tapioca flour, potato starch, dry buttermilk powder, sugar substitute, baking powder, baking soda, salt, and xanthan gum. Stir in eggs, water, and oil until well blended and few lumps remain.

2. Heat a large, well-oiled skillet or griddle over medium high heat. Spoon batter onto skillet and cook until bubbles begin to form. Flip, and continue cooking until golden brown on bottom. Serve immediately with condiments of your choice.

ULTIMATE BREAKFAST CASSEROLE

Servings: 8 | Prep: 15m | Cooks: 45m | Total: 1h

NUTRITION FACTS

Calories: 444 | Carbohydrates: 26.7g | Fat: 37.1g | Protein: 16.7g | Cholesterol: 143mg

INGREDIENTS

- 3 eggs, beaten
- 2 cups cooked ham, cubed
- 1 pinch ground black pepper
- 1 onion, chopped
- 1 (10.75 ounce) can condensed cream of chicken soup
- 3/4 cup shredded Cheddar cheese
- 16 ounces sour cream
- 1/4 cup butter, melted
- 1 (2 pound) package frozen hash brown potatoes, thawed

DIRECTIONS

1. Preheat oven to 350 degrees F (175 degrees C). Lightly grease a 9x13 inch baking dish.
2. Season beaten eggs with pepper; pour into baking dish. In a large bowl, combine soup, sour cream, hash browns, ham, onion and cheese. Mix thoroughly and pour over eggs.
3. Bake uncovered for 30 minutes. Remove and drizzle butter over top of casserole. Return to oven and bake for an additional 15 minutes, until golden.

BROCCOLI QUICHE WITH MASHED POTATO CRUST

Servings: 5 | Prep: 20m | Cooks: 1h15m | Total: 1h35m

NUTRITION FACTS

Calories: 320 | Carbohydrates: 33.5g | Fat: 14.7g | Protein: 14.8g | Cholesterol: 140mg

INGREDIENTS

- 2 large potatoes, peeled
- 1 cup shredded Cheddar cheese

- 2 cups chopped fresh broccoli
- 3 eggs
- 1/4 cup milk
- 1 cup milk
- 1/4 teaspoon salt
- 1/2 teaspoon salt
- 1 tablespoon olive oil
- 1/2 teaspoon ground black pepper
- 1/2 onion, chopped
- 1/4 teaspoon ground nutmeg

DIRECTIONS

1. Preheat oven to 350 degrees F (175 degrees C).
2. Bring a large pot of salted water to a boil. Add potatoes and cook until tender but still firm, about 15 minutes; drain. Meanwhile, place broccoli in a steamer over 1 inch of boiling water, and cover. Cook until tender but still firm, about 2 to 6 minutes. Drain and set aside.
3. Mash the potatoes with milk and salt. Brush a deep 9 inch pie dish with olive oil and press the potatoes in. Brush with remaining olive oil. Bake in preheated oven for 30 minutes or until lightly browned.
4. Arrange onions, broccoli and cheese in the potato crust. Whisk together the eggs, milk, salt, pepper and nutmeg. Pour over broccoli and cheese.
5. Bake in preheated oven for 30 to 40 minutes, until slightly puffed and cooked throughout. Allow to cool for 10 minutes before serving.

PALEO OMELET MUFFINS

Servings: 4 | Prep: 15m | Cooks: 20m | Total: 35m

NUTRITION FACTS

Calories: 308 | Carbohydrates: 6.8g | Fat: 20.5g | Protein: 23.8g | Cholesterol: 403mg

INGREDIENTS

- 8 eggs
- 1/4 teaspoon salt
- 8 ounces cooked ham, crumbled
- 1/8 teaspoon ground black pepper
- 1 cup diced red bell pepper
- 2 tablespoons water
- 1 cup diced onion

DIRECTIONS

1. Preheat oven to 350 degrees F (175 degrees C). Grease 8 muffin cups or line with paper liners.
2. Beat eggs together in a large bowl. Mix ham, bell pepper, onion, salt, black pepper, and water into the beaten eggs. Pour egg mixture evenly into prepared muffin cups.
3. Bake in the preheated oven until muffins are set in the middle, 18 to 20 minutes.

GREAT EASY WAFFLES
Servings: 4 | Prep: 10m | Cooks: 15m | Total: 25m

NUTRITION FACTS

Calories: 505 | Carbohydrates: 61.3g | Fat: 22.5g | Protein: 13.8g | Cholesterol: 158mg

INGREDIENTS

- 2 cups all-purpose flour
- 2 egg yolks
- 2 teaspoons baking powder
- 2 tablespoons grated lemon zest
- 2 tablespoons white sugar
- 1 teaspoon vanilla extract
- 1/2 teaspoon salt
- 2 cups milk
- 2 egg whites
- 6 tablespoons butter, melted

DIRECTIONS

1. Preheat a waffle iron according to manufacturer's instructions.
2. Whisk the flour, baking powder, sugar, and salt together in a mixing bowl; set aside. Beat egg whites until foamy in a separate large glass or metal mixing bowl. Whisk the egg yolks, lemon zest, and vanilla extract together in a third bowl; whisk in the milk. Stir in the flour mixture until smooth. Fold in the melted butter and then the beaten egg whites until just incorporated.
3. Cook the waffles according to manufacturer's instructions until golden brown.

SUPER EASY EGG CASSEROLE
Servings: 4 | Prep: 15m | Cooks: 20m | Total: 35m

NUTRITION FACTS

Calories: 340 | Carbohydrates: 9.3g | Fat: 23.2g | Protein: 23.2g | Cholesterol: 325mg

INGREDIENTS

- 1 cup shredded Cheddar cheese
- 2 green onions, chopped
- 6 eggs, whisked
- 3 tablespoons milk
- 6 slices bacon, diced
- 1/2 teaspoon minced garlic, or to taste (optional)
- 2 slices bread, cubed
- salt and ground black pepper to taste
- 1/3 red bell pepper, diced

DIRECTIONS

1. Preheat oven to 350 degrees F (175 degrees C). Grease a 9x13-inch baking dish.
2. Stir Cheddar cheese, eggs, bacon, bread, red bell pepper, green onion, milk, garlic, salt, and black pepper together in a bowl until well-combined; pour into prepared baking dish.
3. Bake in the preheated oven until eggs are set, 20 to 25 minutes.

Printed in Great Britain
by Amazon